T0303155

HOMELAND SECURITY
OPERATIONAL ANALYSIS CENTER

Logistics Analysis of Puerto Rico

Will the Seaborne Supply Chain of Puerto Rico Support Hurricane Recovery Projects?

ADAM C. RESNICK, ANTHONY DECICCO, VIKRAM KILAMBI, KEENAN D. YOHO,
RAFFAELE VARDAVAS, AARON C. DAVENPORT

Published in 2020

Preface

The research in this report is intended to inform implementation of the Puerto Rico recovery plan, *Transformation and Innovation in the Wake of Devastation: An Economic and Disaster Recovery Plan for Puerto Rico*. Under contract with the Federal Emergency Management Agency (FEMA), the Homeland Security Operational Analysis Center (HSOAC) provided substantial support in developing that recovery plan by soliciting and integrating input from a wide variety of stakeholders, contributing analysis where needed, and supporting drafting of the plan. The plan included an overview of damage and needs, courses of action (COAs) to meet those needs, costs of the COAs, and potential funding mechanisms for those costs.

After completing the recovery plan, HSOAC was tasked to study whether the logistics capacity of Puerto Rico would support the anticipated increase in imports of materials for use in funded recovery projects. The research focused on available capacity to import the materials anticipated to stress the logistics system, large and heavy items. These items are imported to Puerto Rico via the seaborne logistics system. This report should be of interest to FEMA, the government of Puerto Rico, and individuals active in performing work as part of the Puerto Rico recovery plan.

This research was sponsored by FEMA and conducted within the Strategy, Policy, and Operations Program of the HSOAC federally funded research and development center (FFRDC). More information about HSOAC's contribution to planning for recovery in Puerto Rico, along with links to other reports being published as part of this series, can be found at www.rand.org/hsoac/puerto-rico-recovery.

Comments or questions on this draft report should be addressed to the project leaders, Adam Resnick and Anthony DeCicco, at resnick@rand.org and adecicco@rand.org.

About the Homeland Security Operational Analysis Center

The Homeland Security Act of 2002 (Section 305 of Public Law 107-296, as codified at 6 U.S.C. § 185) authorizes the Secretary of Homeland Security, acting through the Under Secretary for Science and Technology, to establish one or more FFRDCs to provide independent analysis of homeland security issues. The RAND Corporation operates HSOAC as an FFRDC for the U.S. Department of Homeland Security (DHS) under contract HSHQDC-16-D-00007.

The HSOAC FFRDC provides the government with independent and objective analyses and advice in core areas important to the department in support of policy development, decisionmaking, alternative approaches, and new ideas on issues of significance. The HSOAC FFRDC also works with and supports other federal, state, local, tribal, and public- and private-sector organizations that make up the homeland security enterprise. The HSOAC FFRDC's research is undertaken by mutual consent with DHS and is organized as a set of discrete tasks. This report presents the results of research and analysis conducted under 70FBR218F00000032, Puerto Rico Economic and Disaster Recovery Plan: Integration and Analytic Support.

The results presented in this report do not necessarily reflect official DHS opinion or policy.

For more information on HSOAC, see www.rand.org/hsoac. For more information on this publication, visit www.rand.org/t/RR3040.

Contents

Figures

Tables

Summary

Concerned by challenges facing the recovery effort in Puerto Rico in the immediate months following Hurricane Maria, which occurred in September 2017, the federal coordinating officer of the Federal Emergency Management Agency (FEMA) recovery effort in Puerto Rico asked the Homeland Security Operational Analysis Center (HSOAC) to study issues related to supply chain management that may arise in fiscal year (FY) 2019, as funds to support recovery projects are disbursed and work is under way.[1] In response, HSOAC began three research tasks to understand what challenges may arise and what could be done to mitigate the challenges. The research in this report was performed as part of the task to understand logistics challenges.

The logistics challenges most anticipated to occur during the execution of recovery projects in Puerto Rico are centered on the requirement to move large, heavy materials onto and then around the main island. In particular, significant challenges could result from degradation of the original transportation network, including remaining damage from Hurricane Maria. Degradation or damage to port resources such as cranes, loaders, or container staging yards could significantly reduce effective container throughput and cause delays. Likewise, damage to bridges or roadways could restrict the flow of recovery resources into some areas of the island. Also, the potentially massive requirement for import and transport of construction materials needed to support simultaneous recovery projects represents another challenge, one that could exacerbate the other logistic challenges.

Recovery Spending in Puerto Rico

The recovery plan for Puerto Rico seeks over $130 billion, to be spent over 11 years, focused on physical investment and other areas.[2] These expenditures were modeled by the HSOAC team for their impact on the economy. A baseline estimate of $10 billion per year was used in HSOAC team economic analysis, with a range between $1 billion and $25 billion per year assessed in the economic analysis to understand what the effect of $130 billion in expenditures would be if there were peaks and valleys in the spending rate over the 11 years.[3]

An additional $10 billion in spending per year on recovery projects in Puerto Rico would be a sizable increase in economic activity, as a percentage of the gross domestic product (GDP).

---

[1] More information about HSOAC's contribution to planning for recovery in Puerto Rico, along with links to other reports being published as part of this series, can be found at www.rand.org/hsoac/puerto-rico-recovery.

[2] Central Office for Recovery, Reconstruction and Resiliency, *Transformation and Innovation in the Wake of Devastation: An Economic and Disaster Recovery Plan for Puerto Rico*, August 8, 2018.

[3] RAND Corporation, "Supporting Puerto Rico's Disaster-Recovery Planning," webpage, Spring 2019.

The Puerto Rico GDP in 2016 was $105 billion.[4] On this basis, $10 billion in annual recovery spending would amount to a nearly 10-percent increase in the economic activity in Puerto Rico.

Input–output analysis generates outputs in terms of dollar spending and employed individuals. Based on the HSOAC team analysis of $10 billion spent on recovery projects, the input–output analysis of the Puerto Rico economy generates projected numbers of additional people employed across industry sectors and employment categories. Notable to the logistics analysis, the input–output model projects that 2,354 additional individuals will need to be employed in the area of heavy and tractor-trailer truck drivers in order for the additional economic activity to be performed. This is a 29-percent increase over the 8,130 individuals determined to be employed in this area in 2017, according to the Bureau of Labor Statistics data that underly input–output models.[5]

As all material that moves through the seaborne supply chain and onward to Puerto Rico destinations does so by truck, this research uses the input–output analysis result of 2,354 additional truck drivers employed as a result of $10 billion in additional spending on recovery projects as the basis for how many additional trucks may be on the road and need to be accommodated by the roadways.

For the port analysis, this research uses the two estimates of increase in economic activity. As a portion of the GDP, the $10 billion in recovery spending represents a near 10-percent increase in activity, which can be considered a conservative assumption about increased demand for materials moving through the ports. However, through the input–output analysis, and acknowledging that the recovery spending may include more consumption of heavy materials than the balance of Puerto Rico economic activity, this research also considers the 29-percent increase in demand for truck drivers as a more liberal assumption (and likely overestimate) of the amount of additional material moving onto the island, through the ports.

It is difficult to estimate the pace at which demand for logistics capacity will increase in Puerto Rico as a result of recovery projects. For recovery projects funded by federal agencies to begin work, requests for funds must be submitted by agencies of the government of Puerto Rico, requests must be approved, contracts must be awarded, and zoning requirements must be met and work plans completed. At the time of this report, only dozens of projects have been submitted to FEMA for approval, out of tens of thousands in damage reported. It is conceivable that the increase in demand for logistics capacity may be gradual, spanning months (or years) before an increase of 10–29 percent is observed, rather than days or weeks.

---

[4] For additional information, please see the recovery plan website (RAND, 2019).

[5] Bureau of Economic Analysis, *RIMS II: An Essential Tool for Regional Developers and Planners*, December 2013.

Ports

The Port of San Juan has been called Puerto Rico's most important piece of infrastructure, given the high reliance on imports (for example, Puerto Rico imports approximately 85 percent of its food, and all liquid fuel).

The Port of San Juan (see Figure S.1) is the largest port for containerized and roll-on/roll-off (RO/RO) cargo (such as cars) on the island. The port is owned by the Puerto Rico Port Authority (PRPA). Three main containerized cargo operators service vessels delivering goods to the port: (1) TOTE Maritime, shipping goods primarily out of Jacksonville, Florida; (2) Crowley Maritime, providing liner service out of Jacksonville, Florida, and Penn Terminal in Philadelphia, Pennsylvania; and (3) Trailer Bridge, providing liner service out of Jacksonville, Florida. There are other, smaller operations, but these three companies handle almost all of the cargo shipping in the Port of San Juan.

Figure S.1. Port of San Juan, Puerto Rico

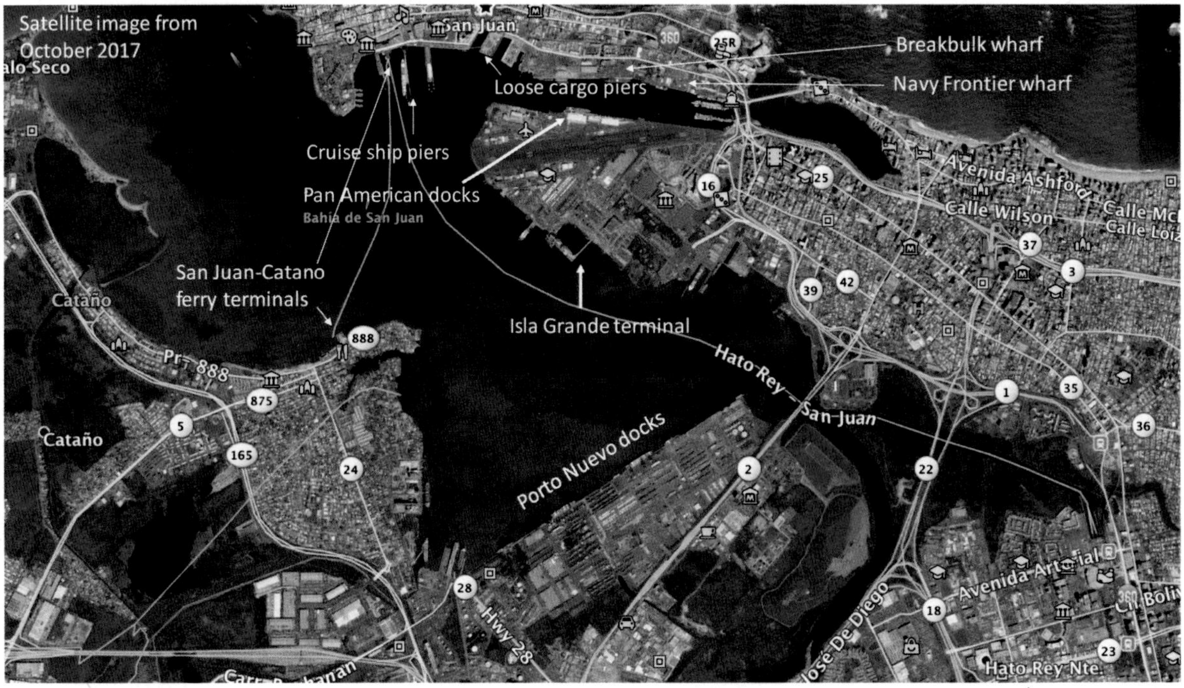

SOURCE: Data from Google Maps.

TOTE Maritime

TOTE Maritime[6] at the Puerto Nuevo docks is the largest Jones Act[7] operator in Puerto Rico. The infrastructure at the Puerto Rico Terminals terminal, the terminal operator for TOTE Maritime, includes the largest facility by acreage, storage volume, and capacity to load and unload ships, with six gantry cranes on 120 acres leased from the PRPA (Figure S.2). The firm provides RO/RO and lift-on/lift-off (LO/LO) cargo services that include dry cargo, refrigerated cargo, hazardous materials, not-in-container cargo, break-bulk boxes, and vehicles.

Figure S.2. Puerto Rico Terminals Terminal, San Juan, Puerto Rico

SOURCE: Data from Google Maps.

TOTE Maritime receives and unloads approximately five ships per week, between ships that it operates and those from international locations. TOTE Maritime performs unloading operations only on days that the ships arrive. While TOTE Maritime has berths and cranes sufficient to unload three or four ships simultaneously, in its current operations there would typically be between zero and two ships in port at the same time.

---

[6] Unless otherwise cited in this section, all information is from an interview with TOTE Maritime, December 2018, Puerto Rico, except for the images, which are from Google.

[7] A shipper that complies with stipulations in the Jones Act, and as a result is permitted to move cargo from a U.S. location to a U.S. location (rather than from a non-U.S. location to a U.S. location, or vice versa). A good summary of the Jones Act implications for Puerto Rico is in this report: U.S. Government Accountability Office, *Puerto Rico, Characteristics of the Island's Maritime Trade and Potential Effects of Modifying the Jones Act*, GAO-13-260, Washington, D.C., March 2013.

Crowley Maritime

Crowley Maritime[8] is the oldest Jones Act firm in Puerto Rico. The terminal operates a "carousel" system for handling containerized cargo, consisting of three quay cranes. The terminal is on 85 acres of leased land (Figure S.3), has three RO/RO ship berths, and eight reach stackers to move containers within the yard. The company provides liner service to the Port of San Juan from Jacksonville, Florida, and Philadelphia, Pennsylvania, the Rio Haina Port in the Dominican Republic, and from St. Thomas and St. Croix. Crowley Maritime receives only its own ships (i.e., those it operates) into the Port of San Juan.

Figure S.3. Crowley Maritime Terminal, San Juan, Puerto Rico

SOURCE: Data from Google Maps.

Crowley unloads five vessels on a weekly basis and one bi-weekly barge, performing unloading operations only on days the ships arrive.

Port Capacity

The primary capacity constraint to moving cargo through the Port of San Juan is the infrastructure of berths and quay cranes. Between TOTE Maritime and Crowley Maritime, the two terminal operators have sufficient berths and cranes to increase by at least 50 percent the

[8] All data from interviews with Crowley Maritime, December 2018, Puerto Rico.

number of ships they receive. Both operators receive ships on several days of the week, and they perform unloading operations only on the day the ships arrive.

The other capacity constraints in the Port of San Juan are the infrastructure of yard space to store containers, and the resources of labor and reach-tuggers to move cargo. Maritime port terminal capacity is planned under the assumption that demand and cargo movement is fairly stable over time; and as private businesses, the port operators do not incur the expense of planning for surges. Therefore, any surge in demand that is due to unpredicted causes or that is outside the planning of the terminal operators will result in a buildup of containers at the port terminals and a slowdown in port throughput.

By their actions in the months following Hurricane Maria in 2017, the terminal operators exhibited their ability to respond to increasing material flow. In the case of the labor and material handling equipment, the private terminal operators Crowley Maritime and TOTE Maritime were able to respond when it became apparent that they would be unable to meet their demands with the resources they had. They leased additional reach-tuggers to meet the increased demands experienced in the posthurricane period, and they were able to recruit sufficient additional laborers from Puerto Rico while bringing in some experienced senior staff from their operations in the continental United States (CONUS). It can be anticipated that the port operators would be able to make similar adjustments to meet increased demand for materials by funded recovery projects. The lead time required to make these adjustments may be a matter of weeks, which would be rapid enough to respond to large increases in demand for logistics capacity owing to recovery projects, if the ramp-up period for the projects is over months (or years).

In the case of additional yard space, the terminal operators do not own the land; they lease it from the PRPA. And it is up to the PRPA to make land or space available for lease, preferably land that is directly adjacent to the current terminal operations so that economies of scale may be realized when it comes to material handling equipment and cargo management and control. Making land available for lease that is off-site or at a distance from current terminal operations creates an additional management and financial burden on the terminal operators and consumes more resources, especially trucks.

Key actions FEMA or the government of Puerto Rico could take to mitigate future delays in port operations would be to coordinate demands for materials to avoid outsize surges in material flow, and communicate changes in future demand to the port operators; make yard space available; and work through interagency efforts to affect the available supply of trucks and truck drivers and the capacity of customers to receive shipments, to avoid delays in customers picking up materials.

Roads

Consisting of approximately 16,500 miles of roadway on an island of 5,300 square miles, Puerto Rico's road network is among the densest in the United States. Of interest is the island's strategic highway network, which is shown in Figure S.4.

Figure S.4. Strategic Highway Network in Puerto Rico

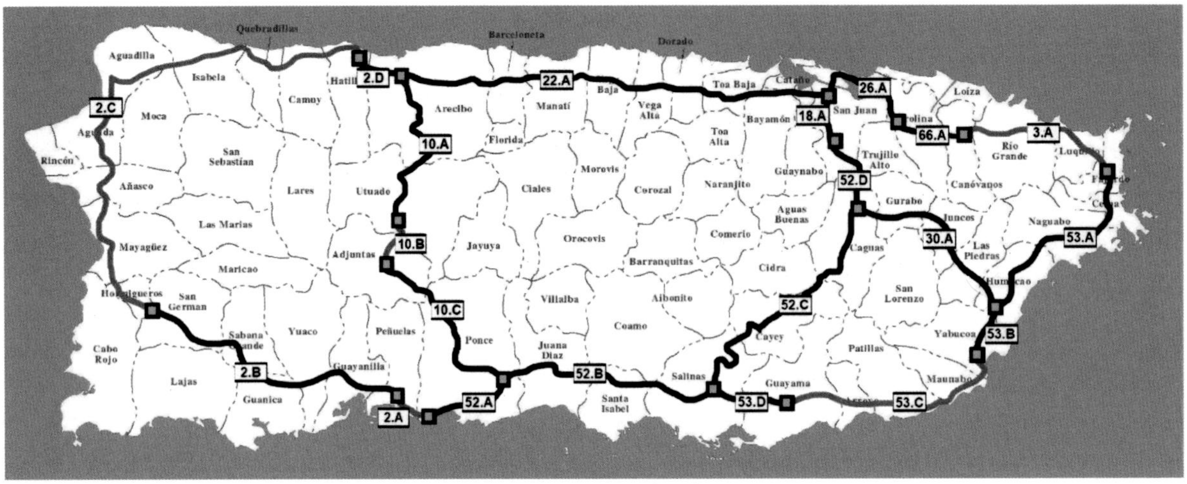

NOTE: Red corresponds to sections that are not completed or require rehabilitation.

This research is structured to analyze by observation the capacity of Puerto Rico roads for moving materials in the first and last miles. The research also includes a trafficability analysis of the strategic distribution network of highways.

First and Last Miles

The research team did not identify any issues with transportation of freight leaving the Port of San Juan, and besides minor delays owing to local traffic conditions in San Juan, the team did not identify any major issues entering the highway network.[9]

While San Juan is the presumed point of origin for the freight, the research team noted some potential difficulties with sending heavy trucks to interior towns such as Lares. For example, one of the most accessible routes to this town from the west involves traveling single-lane, winding, nonsignalized roads at steeply increasing or decreasing elevations (PR-111). Freight arriving to such destinations will have to use lighter trucks in San Juan or transfer material from heavy

---

[9] The research team watched trucks leave the Port of San Juan and join the highway network, in daylight hours and clear weather. The roads allowed two trucks to drive in parallel and enter the highway without traffic delay. This analysis was not inclusive of all the highway entrances or frontage roads in the San Juan area.

trucks to lighter truckers nearer to the destination, potentially adding some delay, inconvenience, and cost.

Travel Speeds on the Strategic Distribution Network

Travel on Puerto Rico's roads, especially outbound from San Juan, is mostly constrained during peak hours. Figure S.5 presents the hours in a typical weekday where speeds are at 70 percent of their maximum or higher. For example, trucks departing from San Juan toward Arecibo would travel fastest along PR-22 West if departing between 8:00 a.m. and 3:00 p.m. or between 7:00 p.m. and 4:00 a.m.

Figure S.5. Times of Weekday with the Fastest Travel Speeds

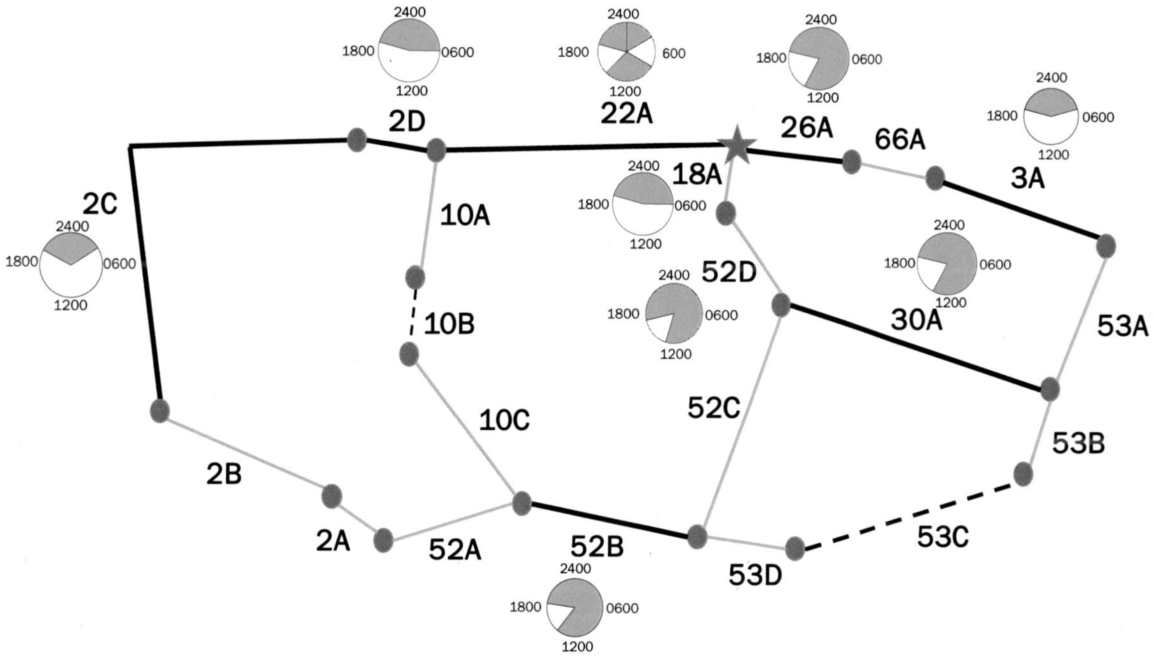

The 24-hour clock figures indicate weekday times when speeds are at least 70% of maximums.
For segments indicated with green lines, speeds at all times are within 70% of maximums.
For segments indicated with dashed lines, data is unavailable.

SOURCE: Data from Google Maps.
NOTE: Highway segments correspond to segments depicted in Figure S.4.

The findings of the analyses indicate that the highways of Puerto Rico possess sufficient capacity to support movement of materials for recovery projects during nonpeak hours. With a baseline estimate of $10 billion in annual recovery project funding, the principal issues will be availability of trucking services, traffic congestion in San Juan and its vicinity, and possibly last mile transportation to interior areas of the island. The findings of the above analyses indicate that except during peak hours, the highway network of Puerto Rico has enough capacity to absorb additional demand caused by recovery efforts without significant delays, with the greatest density around San Juan. Moreover, at current loadings and inventory ratings, most bridges along the highway network should be able to sustain additional traffic, although some will require maintenance soon.

An analysis of sectors across the Puerto Rico economy reveals that enhancing the labor supply will be crucial to supporting recovery efforts.[10] The main requirement at the outset of the recovery will be the availability of truckers, and this should be addressed specifically. Possible policy options include working with U.S. interagency partners such as the Department of Labor, and workforce training, development, and retention programs designed to increase employment of key occupations in Puerto Rico. To support the logistics capacity of Puerto Rico as materials are imported for recovery projects, the availability of trucks and truck drivers is fundamental.

The analysis of potential travel conditions on the road network suggests that coordinating projects will be beneficial. Smoothing material demands for truckers and managing pickups and drop-offs around peak times on roads would improve material throughput and cost.

Recommendations

There are several actions that FEMA could take directly or can facilitate to mitigate the potential problems identified above. HSOAC offers the following recommendations:

- Coordination between FEMA and the port terminal operators may enable the terminal operators to prepare effectively for managing increased container shipments by arranging for access to more material handling equipment (especially reach-tuggers) as soon as it is needed.
- PRPA should make more space available for use as container yard adjacent to or near the Crowley Maritime terminal. Warehouse 21, which is damaged beyond repair, could be taken down and used as yard space. Warehouse 22 could also be taken down and used for container storage during a surge.
- PRPA should also avoid using potential cargo yard space that is near a cargo terminal for debris storage after a natural disaster. Instead, PRPA should find locations away from the port terminals to store garbage and debris, to preserve alternative future options for use of the space by cargo terminals.
- The analysis of potential travel conditions on the road network suggests that coordinating projects will be beneficial. Smoothing material demands for truckers and managing pickups and drop-offs around peak times on roads would improve material throughput and cost of transportation.
- FEMA and U.S. government agencies should focus on workforce capacity building in Puerto Rico, including truck drivers, to address logistics challenges ahead of execution of recovery plan projects.

---

[10] RAND Corporation, Spring 2019.

Acknowledgments

We acknowledge the support and encouragement of our project sponsor Michael Byrne, FEMA's acting Caribbean area division director and the federal coordinating officer and federal disaster-recovery coordinator for Hurricanes Irma and Maria response and recovery in Puerto Rico. He sponsored HSOAC's work in support of the development of the congressionally mandated recovery plan and asked for this supporting analysis to provide context for implementation.

We thank the organizations that participated through discussions, lending their experience working during the posthurricane recovery period, including Crowley Maritime and TOTE Maritime. We also thank the kind and good people of Puerto Rico, who greeted us and directed us as we toured the roads of the island to understand their nature and capacity.

The authors of this report benefited from the input from colleagues who worked on the damage needs assessment of Puerto Rico. Finally, we would like to thank our peer reviewers, Eric Peltz (RAND) and Michael Lowder (Michael W. Lowder and Global Associates, LLC). Their reviews contributed substantially to improving this report.

Abbreviations

AADT	average annual daily traffic
COA	course of action
CONUS	continental United States
DHS	U.S. Department of Homeland Security
DTOP	Departamento de Transportación y Obras Publicias
FEMA	Federal Emergency Management Agency
FFRDC	federally funded research and development center
FFS	free-flow speed
FHWA	Federal Highway Administration
FY	fiscal year
GDP	gross domestic product
HPMS	Highway Performance Monitoring System
HSOAC	Homeland Security Operational Analysis Center
HV	fraction of traffic consisting of heavy trucks
LO/LO	lift-on, lift-off
LOS	level of service
MPH	miles per hour
NBI	National Bridge Inventory
PRPA	Autoridad de los Puertos de Puerto Rico, Puerto Rico Port Authority
PRT	Puerto Rico Terminals
RO/RO	roll-on, roll-off
SEC	structural evaluation code
TEU	twenty-foot equivalent unit

1. Introduction

Concerned by challenges facing the recovery effort in Puerto Rico in the immediate months following Hurricane Maria, which occurred in September 2017, the federal coordinating officer of the Federal Emergency Management Agency (FEMA) recovery effort in Puerto Rico asked the Homeland Security Operational Analysis Center (HSOAC) to study issues related to supply chain management that may hinder the success of hurricane recovery projects, arising in fiscal year (FY) 2019 and onward, as funds to support recovery projects are disbursed and work is under way. In response, HSOAC began three research tasks to understand what challenges may arise and what could be done to mitigate the challenges. The research in this report was performed as part of the task to understand logistics challenges.[1]

In this introduction chapter there are three sections that discuss the scope of the potential logistics challenges research, projected increases in demand for materials in Puerto Rico, and how the ports and roads in Puerto Rico interrelate for the movement of cargo.

Scope of Potential Logistics Challenges

The logistics challenges most anticipated to occur during the execution of recovery projects in Puerto Rico are centered on the requirement to move large, heavy materials onto and then around the main island. The vast majority of materials used in Puerto Rico construction or infrastructure building are imported. The biggest industries in the manufacturing sector in Puerto Rico are biotechnology and pharmaceuticals (bio-pharma), basic chemicals, computer and electronics, medical devices, beverages and tobacco, and food. These industries make up 95 percent of the manufacturing in Puerto Rico (Figure 1.1).[2] So while manufacturing makes up 47 percent of the Puerto Rico gross domestic product (GDP),[3] only a small portion of this may be the large, heavy items demanded by recovery projects.

---

[1] More information about HSOAC's contribution to planning for recovery in Puerto Rico, along with links to other reports being published as part of this series, can be found at www.rand.org/hsoac/puerto-rico-recovery.

[2] The electrical equipment sector (appliances and components) may include heavy items demanded by recovery projects, but it makes up only 1.6 percent of the manufacturing sector, with the remaining 3.3 percent of Puerto Rico manufacturing industries defined as "other" (Puerto Rico Planning Board via Build Back Better, November 2017). [Cited directly from the HSOAC Economics Sector volume.]

[3] Puerto Rico Planning Board, 2016, Table 9. [Cited directly from the HSOAC Economics Sector volume.]

Figure 1.1. Economic Activity in Puerto Rico, FY 2016

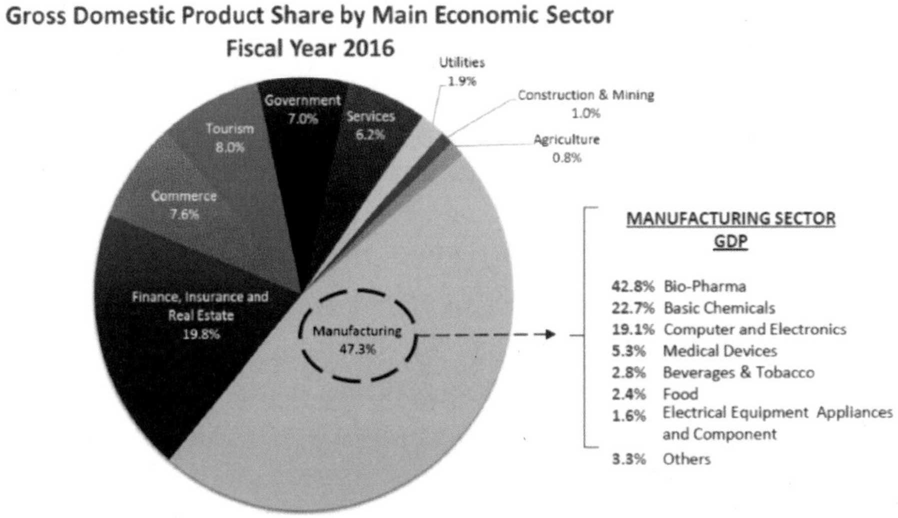

SOURCE: Puerto Rico Planning Board via Build Back Better, 2017.

The large, heavy materials that are imported to Puerto Rico are anticipated to enter the island by the seaborne supply chain. Railways are not used in a major way in Puerto Rico to move cargo, so this research is scoped to analyze the logistics capacity to move materials into Puerto Rico through the ports, and onto onward destinations via the roadways. To further scope the research to focus on the largest portion of demanded materials in Puerto Rico, the analysis was performed only on demand for materials by projects on the main island of Puerto Rico.

The HSOAC team used the approach of a *node-link analysis* to understand the logistics capacity of the Puerto Rico seaborne supply chain. The terminology "node-link" is used to represent a system of connected processes that must occur, in this case to move materials onto the island and to their destinations. The analysis is organized by two areas—ports and roadways. Within the areas of ports and roadways, the capacity to move material is structured around available infrastructure and resources.

The research team took the approach of addressing these questions:

- What is the existing capacity to move additional material along the seaborne supply chain into Puerto Rico?
- What are the logistics challenges that may be faced with the increased import of materials, and how can they be mitigated?

Increased Demand for Materials in Puerto Rico

The recovery plan for Puerto Rico seeks over $130 billion, to be spent over 11 years, focused on physical investment and other areas.[4] The expenditures anticipated over this period to fund

---

[4] Central Office for Recovery, Reconstruction and Resiliency, 2018.

projects associated with the recovery plan were analyzed by the HSOAC team for their impact on the economy. A baseline estimate of $10 billion per year was used for this logistics analysis, with a range between $1 billion and $25 billion per year to understand what the effect of $130 billion in expenditures would be if there were peaks and valleys in the spending rate over the 11 years.[5]

Recovery Spending as a Portion of the Puerto Rico Economy

An additional $10 billion in spending per year on recovery projects in Puerto Rico would be a sizable increase in economic activity, as a percentage of the GDP. The Puerto Rico GDP in 2016 was $105 billion.[6] On this basis, $10 billion in annual recovery spending would amount to a nearly 10-percent increase in the economic activity in Puerto Rico. However, the type of activity represented by the recovery spending would be of a different nature than that of the overall economy—it would be far more heavily focused on construction (which would likely mean a greater than 10-percent increase in large, heavy materials moving onto the island). As shown in Figure 1.1, construction and mining combine to make up only 1 percent of the Puerto Rico economy. The HSOAC team analyzed the courses of action (COAs) in the Puerto Rico Recovery Plan to identify sectors of the economy in which the recovery spending would occur, and determined that 48 percent of spending related to the proposed COAs in the plan would be spent on construction (Table 1.1).

Table 1.1. Mapping from COAs to Sectors and Cost Proportions

Sector	Keywords	Plan Cost (%)
Construction	Built, build, repair, replace	48
Administrative	Incentivize, plan, study, task force, steering committee	39
Management of companies	Business consulting, assist, manage, compensate, improve, implement	12
Educational services	Training, schooling, education	1

SOURCE: RAND Corporation, Spring 2019.

On this basis, the recovery spending in Puerto Rico is projected to amount to a greater than 10-percent increase in the demand for heavy materials, as the spending would be incurred in a sector of the economy that can be assumed to consume heavy materials in its inputs.

---

[5] RAND Corporation, "Supporting Puerto Rico's Disaster-Recovery Planning," webpage, Spring 2019.

[6] Puerto Rico Planning Board, 2016, Table 1. [Cited directly from RAND Corporation, "Supporting Puerto Rico's Disaster-Recovery Planning," Spring 2019.]

Recovery Spending Modeled by Input–Output Analysis of the Puerto Rico Economy

Input–output analysis generates outputs in terms of dollar spending and employed individuals.[7] Based on the HSOAC team analysis of $10 billion spent on the industries represented in Table 1.1, the input–output analysis of the Puerto Rico economy generates projected numbers of additional people employed across industry sectors and employment categories.[8] Notable to the logistics analysis, the input–output model projects that 2,354 additional individuals will need to be employed in the area of heavy and tractor-trailer truck drivers in order for the additional economic activity to be performed. This is a 29-percent increase over the 8,130 individuals determined to be employed in this area in 2017, according to the Bureau of Labor Statistics data that underly the input–output models.[9] Input–output models are linear, which is to say that if 2,354 truck drivers are determined to be employed with an additional $10 billion in activity, then 2,354 × 2.5 or 5,885 additional truck drivers would be employed if there were recovery spending in Puerto Rico at the rate of $25 billion per year. Not all of these truckers will be employed moving cargo into Puerto Rico, but a sizable portion will.

Use of Recovery Spending Calculations in This Research

Because material that moves through the seaborne supply chain and onward to Puerto Rico destinations does so by truck, this research uses the input–output analysis result of 2,354 additional truck drivers employed as a result of $10 billion in additional spending on recovery projects as a basis to estimate how many additional trucks may be on the road and need to be accommodated by the roadways.

---

[7] Input–output analysis accounts for three types of effects on an economy: direct, indirect, and induced. The direct effect of spending $10 billion × 48 percent of recovery funds on construction yields a direct effect of $4.8 billion in construction activity in Puerto Rico. The Bureau of Economic Analysis data that underly an input–output model is specific to a region (in this case Puerto Rico). The data describe how much local output from other industries is consumed as input to generate $4.8 billion in construction activity in Puerto Rico, such as spending on local services, transportation and warehousing, and households (labor). This additional spending is called the indirect effect and added to the direct effect to calculate the total economic effect. In addition, the model accounts for further spending effects, such as spending by households employed in the construction activity; these are called induced effects.

In accompanying reports, the HSOAC team calculated the total effect of $10 billion in spending on recovery COAs in Puerto Rico would result in an additional $17.5 billion in economic activity. The team calculated the total yield in additional employment would be 210,000 members of households. The two largest affected occupation categories experience increases of 34,900 members employed in office and administrative support occupations, and 31,700 members employed in construction and extraction occupations. Notable for this logistics research, 18,200 members will be employed in transportation and material moving occupations, which includes 2,354 employed heavy and tractor-trailer truck drivers.

Additional references on input–output models can be found at IMPLAN.com and the Bureau of Economic Analysis, *RIMS II: An Essential Tool for Regional Developers and Planners*, December 2013.

[8] RAND Corporation, Spring 2019.

[9] Bureau of Economic Analysis, December 2013.

For the port analysis, this research uses the two estimates of increase in economic activity. As a portion of the GDP, the $10 billion in recovery spending represents a near 10-percent increase in activity, which can be considered a conservative assumption about increased demand for materials moving through the ports. However, through the input–output analysis, and acknowledging that the recovery spending may include more consumption of heavy materials than the balance of Puerto Rico economic activity, this research also considers the 29-percent increase in demand for truck drivers to be an indication of the increase in material moving onto the island. Anticipating that the increased economic activity will be heavily in construction, which currently represents only 1 percent of the economy of Puerto Rico, we suggest that the increase in material moved through the ports may be higher than 10 percent and closer to the 29-percent estimate.

It is difficult to estimate the pace at which demand for logistics capacity will increase in Puerto Rico as a result of recovery projects. For recovery projects funded by federal agencies to begin work, requests for funds must be submitted by agencies of the government of Puerto Rico, requests must be approved, contracts must be awarded, and zoning requirements must be met and work plans completed. At the time of this report, only dozens of projects have been submitted to FEMA for approval, out of tens of thousands in damage reported. It is conceivable that the increase in demand for logistics capacity may be gradual, spanning months (or years) before an increase of 10–29 percent is observed, rather than days or weeks.

Interdependence of Ports and Roads

Without loss of generality, ports can be conceptualized as being made up of two distinct processes with respect to containerized cargo: (1) off-loading containers from ships and (2) loading containers onto trucks. Port operators use staging areas to store cargo until it is ready to move onward.

When cargo moves swiftly and consistently through a port, little storage space may be necessary. However, when flow out of a port is reduced for any reason, more use of staging areas is required. When cargo remains in the storage yard longer, more of it will accumulate. As a result, if cargo is stored more densely, an increasing number of containers may need to be moved and repositioned before an intended container can be loaded onto a truck, causing trucks to wait for cargo.

Recursively, if trucks are not arriving promptly to pick up cargo when it arrives in the port, the cargo will spend more time at the port waiting for a truck.

2. Ports

Puerto Rico relies on maritime shipping to maintain daily life, economic activity, and government services. Virtually anything that cannot economically fit in the belly of an airplane must be moved via maritime conveyance to and from Puerto Rico's ports.

This chapter of the report contains an overview of the ports on the island, focusing on the three ports that receive cargo, and mainly on the Port of San Juan. The chapter also includes an estimate of the capacity of the port to receive cargo, and its ability to increase capacity.

In this chapter we refer to the actions by the terminal operators in the period after Hurricane Maria. The operators were forced to respond to a large increase in demand for goods, with relief supplies sent. The operators were also faced with customers not picking up cargo that had already been demanded, owing to disaster-related challenges. By their actions after Hurricane Maria, we can understand the means the terminal operators use to increase their capacity, and we can estimate to what level they can increase capacity in response to cargo arriving to support recovery projects.

Overview of Ports on the Main Island

The three cargo ports in Puerto Rico are the Port of San Juan, owned by the Puerto Rico Port Authority (PRPA); the Port of Ponce (Port of the Americas), owned by the Municipality of Ponce; and the Port of Mayaguez, owned by the Mayaguez Port Commission. San Juan was the main cargo port; it handled 99 percent of the total cargo movement as measured in both containers and metric tons between 2014 and 2017.[1] All of the ports in Puerto Rico are shown in Figure 2.1, including those used for cargo and other types of craft.[2]

The Port of San Juan has been called Puerto Rico's most important piece of infrastructure, given the high reliance on imports (for example, Puerto Rico imports approximately 85 percent of its food, and all liquid fuel). Ships use the balance of ports in Puerto Rico for a number of purposes other than cargo.

Figure 2.2 shows the total vessel port arrivals by type and location over the entire three-year period (2015–2017). While other ports in Puerto Rico are active for purposes other than cargo (petroleum in Guayanilla, and passengers between Fajardo and Vieques), only the port in San Juan is used for cargo on a large scale.

---

[1] U.S. Department of Transportation Maritime Administration, "U.S. Waterborne Foreign Container Trade by U.S. Customs Ports 2000–2017," 2017.

[2] RAND Corporation, Spring 2019.

Figure 2.1. Seaports in Puerto Rico

SOURCE: RAND Corporation, Spring 2019.

Figure 2.2. Vessel Types Across All Ports, 2015–2017

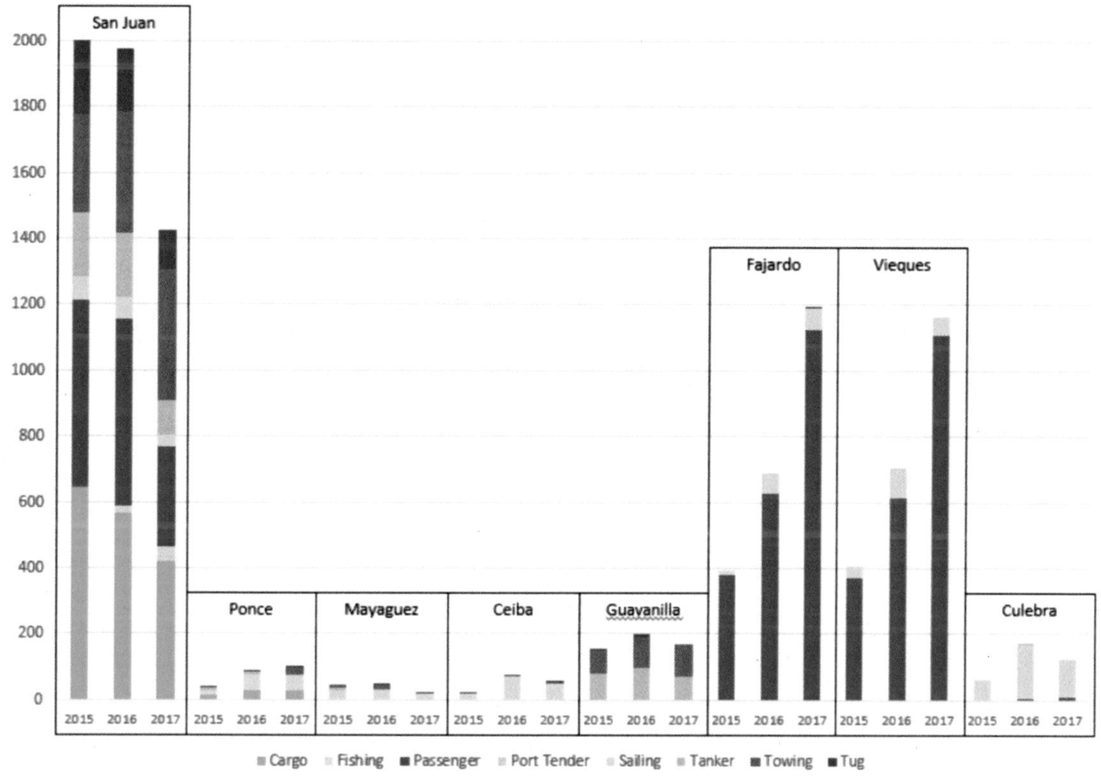

SOURCE: RAND Corporation, Spring 2019.

Utility of the Three Main Cargo Ports

The three ports capable of handling cargo are San Juan, Mayaguez, and Ponce. To understand the utility of the ports, it is important to understand how the population of the island is distributed geographically, and the geographic distribution of demand for goods. Figure 2.3 shows the population density of the island according to the 2000 U.S. census. While Mayaguez and Ponce are near urban areas, the majority of the population of Puerto Rico is along the northern shore, as is the associated majority of demand for goods.[3]

Figure 2.3. Puerto Rico Population Density

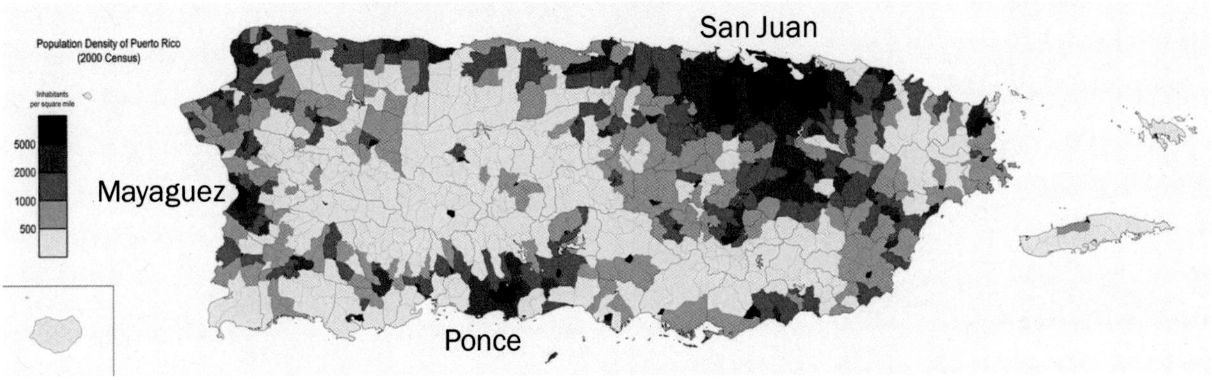

SOURCE: Javier Rodriguez Galarza via Wikipedia, based on data from the U.S. Census Bureau, 2000.

The container volume of cargo shipped through ports in Puerto Rico from 2000 to 2017, measured in twenty-foot equivalent units (TEUs), is given in Figure 2.4. It is clear from the data that, by 2017, the Port of San Juan was the only port on the island that handled any significant cargo volume.

Information and analysis about the utility of the Ports of Mayaguez, Ponce, and San Juan are included in the following sections. Within these sections, and particularly in the in-depth analysis of the Port of San Juan, the capacity of the ports is described in terms of *infrastructure* and *resources*. Infrastructure is defined for this purpose as being capacity-generating aspects of a port terminal that are not easy to expand marginally, such as berths, quay cranes, and total yard space. Resources are defined as those aspects that can be more readily adjusted in the short term with application of funds, such as material handling equipment and labor.

---

[3] After goods arrive in the port, their destination is often to retailers or distribution centers. From interviews with shippers in Puerto Rico, the research team learned that the majority of demand for goods is along the northern shore, and most distribution centers for goods are in the San Juan area.

Figure 2.4. Container Volume Measured in TEUs at the Ports of San Juan, Mayaguez, and Ponce from 2000 to 2017

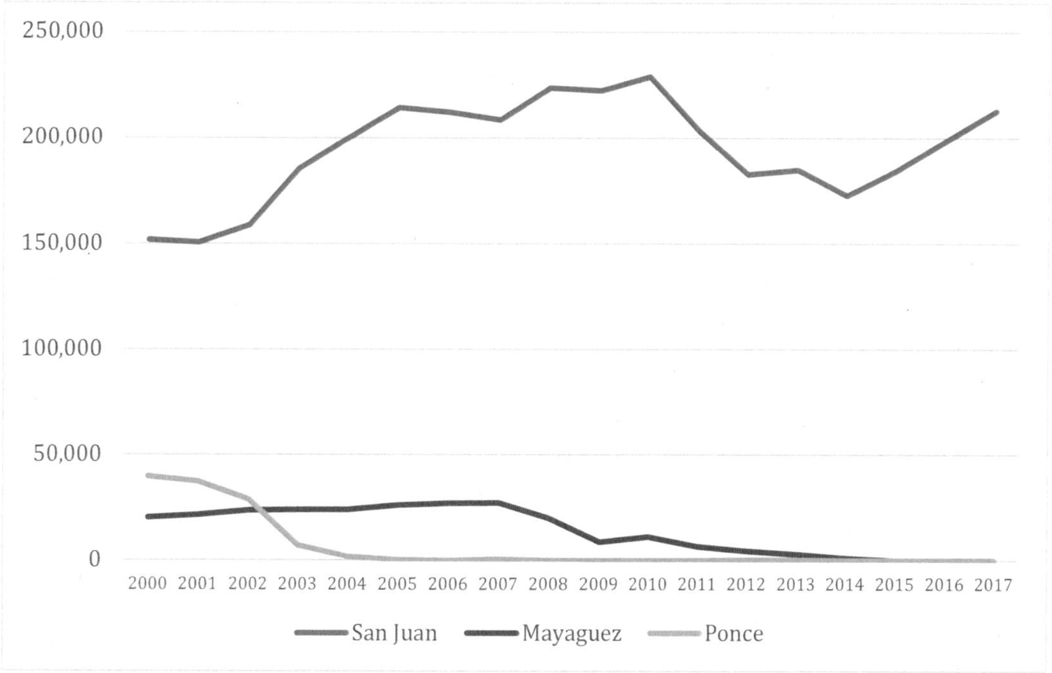

Port of Mayaguez

The Port of Mayaguez (Figure 2.5), on the central and western part of the island, adjacent to the Mona Passage and protected from the Atlantic, has not handled any significant volume since 2014. There are no container cranes at the port and minimal yard space (approximately four acres) for container storage at the terminal. Information on the continual presence of labor and material handling equipment to move cargo was not gathered by the research team; when cargo shipments are unloaded or loaded at the port, they can be moved by resources arranged by customers to be present.

Figure 2.5. Port of Mayaguez

SOURCE: Data from Google Maps.

Port of Ponce

The Port of Ponce[4] (Figure 2.6) is a deep-water port with a 55-foot channel draft, which is an uncommon depth among Caribbean ports. For infrastructure, it has approximately 26 acres of on-site yard space and two nonfunctioning quay cranes. Until recently there were four cranes located at the port, none of them functional in years, but two are all that remain after the other two cranes were dismantled. There are approximately 20–26 employees of the port, 13 of which are security guards. There are six pieces of material handling equipment, or movable cranes, at the port. In discussions with operators of terminals in the Port of San Juan, they said they would use the Port of Ponce in special instances where a customer demanded cargo that was better moved through Ponce than through San Juan (such as where the customer is on the south shore of the island, and the item is oversize or otherwise difficult to move over land), but in these cases the port operator would bring its own workers and use its own cranes.

[4] Information was gathered in an April 2018 interview with Port of Ponce Authority. Image data are from Google.

Figure 2.6. Port of Ponce

SOURCE: Data from Google Maps.

There have been many attempts to develop the port into a transshipment container hub, but with more than $300 million invested over the past decade,[5] there are no cargo ships using the port on a regular basis. Ponce is on the southern coast of the island, which may advantage it to be sheltered from conditions that may affect the northern coast. However, Ponce is distant from the heavily populated northern shore of the island and the distribution centers around San Juan. To move a container by truck from the Port of Ponce to a location near San Juan costs $300 more than moving a container from the Port of San Juan.[6] The current strategic plan at the port is to dismantle the nonfunctioning equipment and sell the scrap metal. Satellite imagery shows scrapping operations currently taking place at the port (see Figure 2.7).

---

[5] R. Pipoli, "Puerto Rico's Ponce Port Completes $250 Million Upgrade, Eyes Caribbean Market," *Latin Business Daily*, September 7, 2015; Port of the Americas, "About the Project," December 7, 2011.

[6] Per interviews with Puerto Rico port operators, Crowley Maritime and TOTE Maritime, Puerto Rico, December 2018.

Figure 2.7. Container Crane Being Scrapped at the Port of Ponce

SOURCE: Data from Google Maps.

The investment in the Port of Ponce in 2015 yielded infrastructure possessed by the Port of Ponce Port Authority, and in anticipation of a market demand for its use. This type of port infrastructure development is different from that performed at the Port of San Juan. In San Juan, the PRPA leases only the land to the terminal operators, and the terminal operators have invested the capital to bring large gantry cranes, material handling equipment, and other improvements to the site. The operators made these investments in order to meet their own shipping demands (as the terminal operators are also the Jones Act carriers bringing cargo from the continental United States [CONUS]), and in the case of TOTE Maritime to economically service the international shippers whose ships it unloads at its terminal in the Port of San Juan.

Port of San Juan

The Port of San Juan (see Figure 2.8) is the largest and only active port for containerized and roll-on/roll-off (RO/RO) cargo (such as cars) on the island. The port is owned by the PRPA. Three main containerized cargo operators service vessels delivering goods to the port: (1) TOTE Maritime, shipping goods primarily out of Jacksonville, Florida; (2) Crowley Maritime, providing liner service out of Jacksonville, Florida, and Penn Terminal in Philadelphia, Pennsylvania; and (3) Trailer Bridge, providing liner service out of Jacksonville, Florida. There are other, smaller operations, but these three companies handle almost all of the cargo shipping in the Port of San Juan. TOTE, Crowley, and Trailer Bridge all provide chassis for container shipping, which means that a truck driver can drive into the port yard area and connect directly to a chassis that has been staged, ready to drive away, with the intended container. As a result—and to support firms adopting just-in-time or lean inventory postures—cargo can be on the shelf at a retailer or in a production facility within 12 hours of a ship docking.[7]

Figure 2.8. Port of San Juan, Puerto Rico

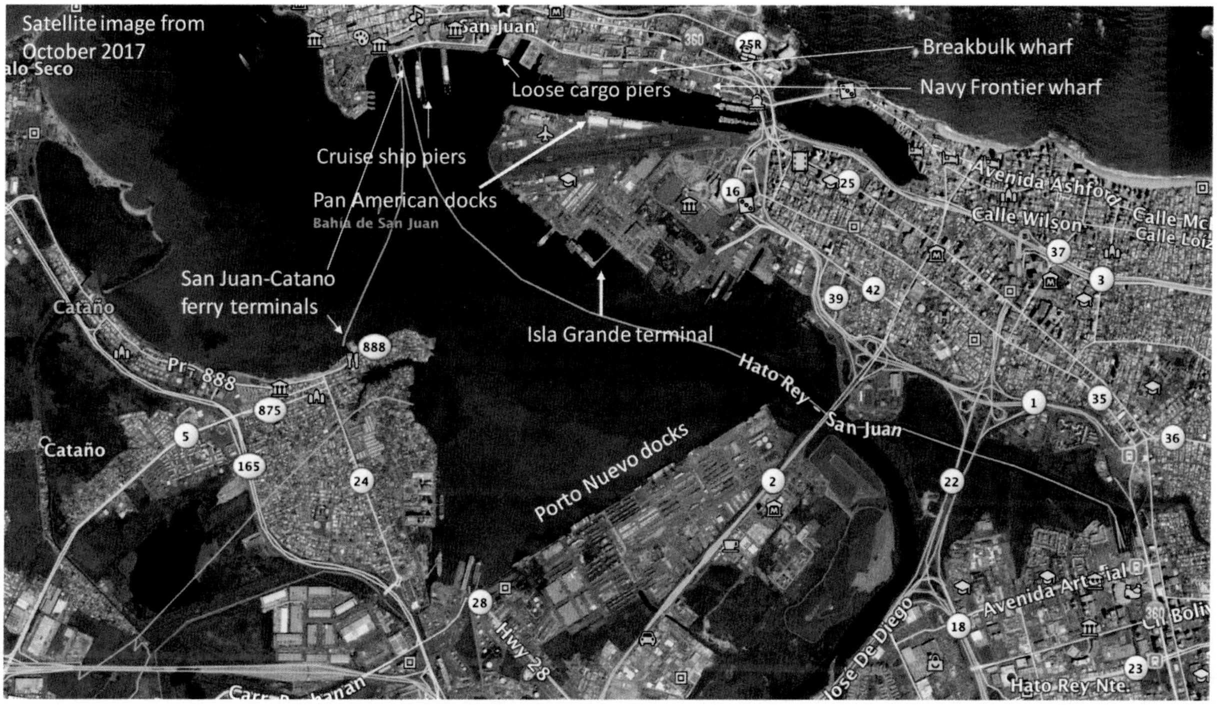

SOURCE: Data from Google Maps.

TOTE Maritime

TOTE Maritime[8] at the Puerto Nuevo docks is the largest Jones Act[9] operator in Puerto Rico. The infrastructure at the Puerto Rico Terminals (PRT) terminal, the terminal operator for TOTE Maritime, includes the largest facility by acreage, storage volume, and capacity to load and unload ships, with seven gantry cranes on 120 acres leased from the PRPA (Figure 2.9 and Figure 2.10). The firm provides RO/RO and lift-on/lift-off (LO/LO) cargo services that include dry cargo, refrigerated cargo, hazardous materials, not-in-container cargo, break-bulk boxes, and vehicles.

---

[7] Per interviews with Puerto Rico shippers, October 2018, Crowley Maritime and TOTE Maritime, Puerto Rico, December 2018.

[8] Unless otherwise cited in this section, all information is from an interview with TOTE Maritime, Puerto Rico, December 2018, except for the images, which are from Google.

[9] A shipper that complies with stipulations in the Jones Act, and as a result is permitted to move cargo from a U.S. location to a U.S. location (rather than from a non-U.S. location to a U.S. location, or vice versa). A good summary of the Jones Act implications for Puerto Rico is in U.S. Government Accountability Office, 2013.

The principal capital and land resources of the Puerto Rico Terminals terminal are given in Table 2.1.

Figure 2.9. Puerto Rico Terminals Terminal, San Juan, Puerto Rico

SOURCE: Data from Google Maps.

Figure 2.10. Puerto Rico Terminals Terminal Details, San Juan, Puerto Rico

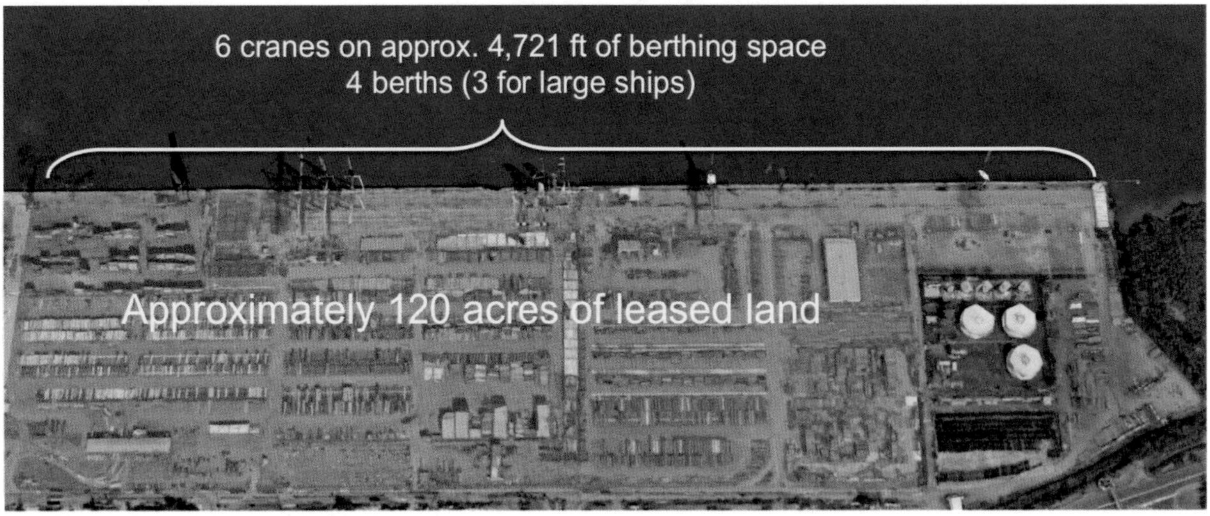

SOURCE: Data from Google Maps.

Table 2.1. Infrastructure (and Material Handling Equipment) at Puerto Rico Terminals Terminal in the Port of San Juan

Feature	Quantity
Yard acreage (leased)	200
Berths	4 (3 for larger ships)
Gantry cranes	7
Reach stackers, also known as top loaders or reach-tuggers	15

All capital assets on the leased land are owned by Puerto Rico Terminals, including the gantry cranes and the reach stackers, which are the material handling equipment used to move the containers from the quayside to yard storage and from yard storage onto chassis and trucks.

There are two ships, operated by TOTE Maritime, that arrive per week from U.S. locations. They arrive on Monday and Friday and are unloaded on those days. Most of the container volume is in 53-foot containers, as all the cargo that leaves the yard does so on trucks, and 53-foot trucks are designed to maximize the amount that can be carried by truck in a single container but still conform to regulations of the U.S. road system. The terminal can also handle a standard 40-foot container (which is the standard set for international use by the International Standards Organization [ISO], hence the name *ISO container*) as well as 50-foot containers. TOTE handles more refrigerated containers ("reefers") than any other terminal on the island, and these containers are all 40 ft in length. The company has generator sets that attach to the containers and create electricity to run the refrigeration systems. Puerto Rico Terminals also unloads ships that it does not own; these ships arrive from international locations.

Puerto Rico Terminals receives and unloads approximately five ships per week, between ships that it operates and those from international locations. Puerto Rico Terminals has berths and cranes sufficient to unload three or four ships simultaneously, in its current operations there would typically be between 0 and 2 ships in port at the same time.

Puerto Rico Terminals Damage and Recovery

Hurricane Maria inflicted approximately $4 million in damage to the gantry cranes at the Puerto Rico Terminals terminal. Two of the cranes are electrically powered and required the use of two temporary generators to be operational during the aftermath. These two cranes make up approximately 70–80 percent of the crane capacity in the terminal. The other cranes are diesel powered.

Because of a shortage of truck drivers,[10] shortages of fuel,[11] and the inability of customers such as large retailers to take receipt of goods, after the storm there was little capacity to transport containers from the terminal area to customer sites. Ships continued to arrive at the port, after journeys begun days or weeks earlier, and containers immediately began stacking up at the terminal. The reasons for retailers not being able to take receipt of their goods included severely damaged facilities (collapsed roofs, broken glass) and lack of electricity to keep perishables cold, among others.

As containers stacked up at the port in the months following the hurricanes in 2017, PRT leased an additional three reach stackers ("top loaders" or "reach-tuggers") to handle the additional volume of container moves required. The lease cost for a single reach stacker is approximately $11,000 per month, and the company needed the equipment for 14 months until it had worked off the queue.

Approximately $3 million was spent to pave areas and harden the surface of the PRT yard to accommodate operations in the months following the 2017 hurricanes. The combined weight of a container and reach-tugger is approximately 300,000 pounds (170,000 pounds for the reach-tugger and 130,000 pounds for the 40- or 53-foot container). Soft ground cannot bear this much weight without sinking, especially with repeated movement. Also, the ground was damaged when containers were stacked several high, placing a large amount of weight on the corner points. The combined and focused weight of stacked containers damaged ground that was previously used to store individual containers on chassis.[12]

Containers dwelled longer not only at the port but also at the customer locations. Many retailers suffered damage to their stores and/or were without electricity for perishable goods. Because the customer locations do not have cranes to remove the containers from the chassis, the chassis dwell times at customer sites also increased. This resulted in a shortage of chassis at the terminals, as well as a shortage of containers in circulation to be returned to Jacksonville to be packed with more goods. Because the terminals rely on a conservation of flow between chassis and containers coming in and going out, any disruption to this flow quickly manifests as shortages and causes further slowdowns in the movement of goods. TOTE Maritime also leased electricity generators and storage banks to maintain constant power to the increased number of reefers in the storage yard.

---

[10] Camila Domonoske, "In Puerto Rico, Containers Full of Goods Sit Undistributed at Ports," *National Public Radio*, September 28, 2017; Dawn Giel, Contessa Brewer, and Lori Ann LaRocco, "Puerto Rico, Short on Fuel, Cannot Deliver Food and Medicine to the Victims of Hurricane Maria," *CNBC*, September 28, 2017.

[11] Bo Erickson, "After Hurricane Maria, Fuel Requests by Walmart Stores in Puerto Rico Went Unanswered," *CBS News*, 2017.

[12] Several weeks after the hurricane struck, there were 390 containers of packaged water at the terminal but no trucks arriving at the yard to move it.

Puerto Rico Terminals Bottleneck Management

Puerto Rico Terminals increased its terminal throughput capacity in three fundamental ways: (1) The company increased its gate hours for trucks by an additional 13 hours per week; (2) the company leased three additional reach-tuggers to handle the surge in inbound containers associated with the emergency efforts, as well as to manage the additional number of container moves associated with the denser storage; and (3) the company added more workers as they were available, with an accommodation from the labor union. The additional workers added to the terminal were primarily temporary general laborers who were not skilled with operating heavy equipment. The unskilled workers were less productive than trained staff: the daily output of a skilled worker took 18 hours by an unskilled one, resulting in additional slowdowns in throughput at the terminal. The increase in work capacity is described in Table 2.2.

Table 2.2. Working Hours, Crane Moves, Truck Gate Moves, and Container Dwell Time Before and After Hurricane Maria

	Prehurricane	Posthurricane
Working hours	50 hours per week Monday–Friday: 7 a.m.–4 p.m. Saturday: 7 a.m.–12 p.m.	63 hours per week Monday–Sunday: 7 a.m.–9 p.m.
Crane moves per week (reported)	5,000	6,300
Truck gate moves per week (reported)	3,500	5,000
Container dwell time (reported)	1.5 days	3.5 days (as many as 20 days)

Crowley Maritime

Crowley Maritime[13] is the oldest Jones Act firm in Puerto Rico. The terminal operates a "carousel" system for handling containerized cargo, consisting of three quay cranes. The terminal is on 85 acres of leased land (Figure 2.11 and Figure 2.12), has three RO/RO ship berths, and eight reach stackers to move containers within the yard (see Table 2.3). The company provides liner service to the Port of San Juan from Jacksonville, Florida, and Philadelphia, Pennsylvania, the Rio Haina Port in the Dominican Republic, and from St. Thomas and St. Croix. Crowley Maritime receives only its own ships (i.e., those it operates) into the Port of San Juan.

Crowley unloads approximately three ships per week, performing unloading operations only on days the ships arrive.

[13] All data from interviews with Crowley Maritime, Puerto Rico, December 2018.

Figure 2.11. Crowley Maritime Terminal, San Juan, Puerto Rico

SOURCE: Data from Google Maps.

Figure 2.12. Crowley Maritime Terminal Details, San Juan, Puerto Rico

SOURCE: Data from Google Maps.

Table 2.3. Capital Machinery, Land, and Berth Space That Constitute the Physical Capacity for the Crowley Maritime Terminal

Resource	Quantity
Yard acreage (leased)	85
Berths	3
Gantry cranes	3
Reach stackers, top loaders, or reach-tuggers	8

Crowley Maritime Damage and Recovery

Crowley's Isla Grande terminal sustained minor damage after the storm.[14] The company established a flow of relief cargo within 48 hours, and its terminal was running normal operating hours within 72 hours. One of the immediate shortages experienced at the Crowley terminal was the shortage of trucks. Trucks cannot run without diesel fuel, and gas stations could not pump diesel fuel because they did not have electricity. There were also difficulties finding drivers for the vehicles—some were unable to get to the port because of blocked roadways. Finally, many of the staff, including drivers, needed to take care of their families at home and could not immediately begin work. Bringing drivers from the U.S. mainland was not considered a viable solution to the shortage according to Crowley, as those drivers are typically not familiar with Puerto Rico's road network. This makes navigation difficult, especially when many road signs were blown away as a result of the hurricane.

The unavailability of trucks soon created container overcrowding problems at the Crowley terminal, especially with the increased demand just after the hurricane. Immediately following the hurricane, there were several ships and barges awaiting U.S. Coast Guard authorization to open the San Juan Bay. Once the bay was officially opened, ships and barges arrived at the port terminal in what was described as a "tsunami of cargo." Within the first month, 4,000 containers arrived, but none left the terminal. At one point, Crowley had 5,000 containers in the yard. Containers had to be stacked vertically in rows for storage. The container density at the terminal was typically 4 or 5 rows of containers single-stacked, but at its peak there were containers parked in rows 22 containers wide, stacked 5 high. When trucks arrived to pick up specific containers, significant sorting and unstacking were required to access the needed container for transport off the port. In spite of measures taken to speed up operations, the Crowley yards were crowded beyond normal levels for almost six months. The primary cause of congestion at the port terminal was due to commercial industry not being able to receive cargo at their retail locations; retailers suffering from physical damage and/or power outages were not receiving cargo. For example, supermarkets did not want to pull refrigerated merchandise to a location without power when those goods in refrigerated containers ("reefers") could stay plugged into the Crowley terminal on their self-sustained power grid. Another complication was that much of the cargo that FEMA had

[14] "Crowley Establishes Flow of Relief Cargo into Puerto Rico Following Hurricane Maria," *Crowley Maritime*, September 22, 2017.

shipped to the port was marked simply "relief cargo," with no other details. This resulted in terminal personnel having to open numerous containers, create a separate manifest, and document the inventory of the container, a requirement to know where to find the contained goods when a truck arrives to retrieve and deliver them. This cargo was typically cleared within 24 to 48 hours and sent to a Crowley staging yard in Bayamon. However, lacking specific details of container cargo on a manifest, terminal personnel had to open numerous containers, create a separate manifest, and document the inventory of the container. This resulted in additional labor hours that would otherwise be used for cargo handling and processing. A detailed manifest of the goods inside a container is a requirement to know where to find the those goods when a truck arrives to retrieve and deliver them, particularly when there is a specific, urgent request. Containers filled with like commodities were much easier to handle as they were moved to the Bayamon staging yard and segregated by commodity type. During the first month of operations after the hurricane made landfall, it took 1 hour and 30 minutes to dispatch a container, a process that involves requesting the container, waiting while it is found and loaded, checking out at the gate, and exiting the terminal. Under normal conditions, typical dispatching time is 18 minutes.

Crowley Maritime Bottleneck Management

To help relieve the bottlenecks at its terminal, Crowley leased an additional ten acres of yard space outside its port terminal space. The company was unable to lease space closer to its terminal because the PRPA used the adjacent space to stack debris. Crowley also purchased two more reach-tuggers for handling containers in the yard and increased scheduled operations from five-day workweeks to seven-day workweeks. The terminal operated during daylight hours for 22 straight days without interruption during the immediate aftermath of the storm. The increase in work capacity is described in Table 2.4.

Table 2.4. Working Hours, Crane Moves, Truck Gate Moves, and Container Dwell Time Before and After Hurricane Maria

	Prehurricane	Posthurricane
Working hours	46.5 hours per week Monday–Friday: 7 a.m.–3:30 p.m. Saturday: 7 a.m.–11 a.m.	63 hours per week Monday–Sunday: 7 a.m.–9 p.m.
Crane moves per week (estimated)	2,500	3,200
Truck gate moves per week (reported)	1,000	1,800
Container dwell time (reported)	1.5 days	3.5 days (as many as 20 days)

Trailer Bridge

Trailer Bridge has approximately 16 acres of yard space that will hold approximately 430 53-foot trailers on chassis (Figure 2.13 and Figure 2.14).[15] The terminal does not have any quay cranes

[15] The research team did not make a site visit to Trailer Bridge.

and handles RO/RO trailer cargo only. Its resources, including labor and material handling equipment, are unknown to the research team.

Figure 2.13. Trailer Bridge Terminal at the Port of San Juan

SOURCE: Data from Google Maps.

Figure 2.14. Trailer Bridge Terminal at the Port of San Juan with Highlighted Yard Acreage

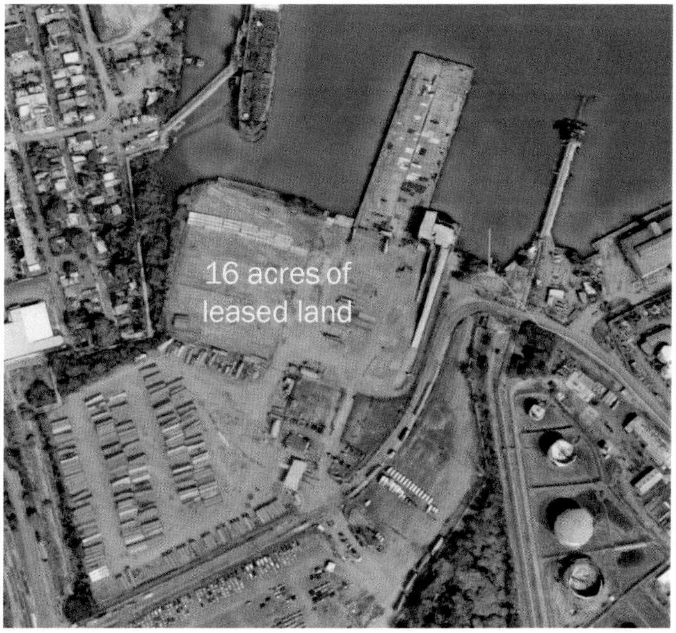

SOURCE: Data from Google Maps.

Estimating the Port of San Juan Capacity

Researchers use many different means of estimating port capacity at various stages of cargo movement from ship to shore, and it is commonly understood that no single, definitive means of estimating the capacity of a port terminal exists.[16] However, there are some key physical determinants of port terminal capacity that, combined with hours of operation, can provide good indicators of total throughput capacity. The principal components of port terminal capacity are

- container yard depth
- container stacking height
- draft of the berthing area
- length of the berthing area
- terminal operating hours.

These components determine the capacity of the terminal to move a container from a ship to the shore. Each component has its own capacity in terms of movement or volume. For example, the ideal yard utilization for a container terminal is commonly held to be 70 percent—handling times increase significantly anytime the yard utilization goes above this level, because congestion develops.[17]

In addition to these estimates, gate moves, or the number of trucks that exit the terminal gates with a container, are a good overall indicator of throughput capacity. We evaluate the capacity of each of the major terminals at the Port of San Juan to process containers from ship to shore. However, we estimate the total capacity of the port by the number of gate moves, which is an indicator of the flow capacity to move a container once it is called for by a customer to be picked up and processed out of the terminal and on to its final destination.

The principal components of port capacity are quay cranes, ground container handling equipment, and yard acreage. The ability to process trucks through the gates once the cargo is unloaded is the final component and defines the throughput. The estimated component capacity for crane moves, container handling, yard acreage, and truck gate moves for each major terminal operator are shown in Figure 2.15, which illustrates the typical flow of containerized cargo to the Port of San Juan.

---

[16] S. Hartmann, J. Pohlmann, and A. Schönknecht, "Simulation of Container Ship Arrivals and Quay Occupation," in J. Böse, ed., *Handbook of Terminal Planning*, New York: Springer, 2011, pp. 135–154.

[17] I. N. Lagoudis and J. Rice, Jr., "Revisiting Port Capacity: A Practical Method for Investment and Policy Decisions," Proceedings, ECONSHIP, Chios, Greece, 2011.

Figure 2.15. Estimated Component Capacities for the Three Major Terminal Operators at the Port of San Juan

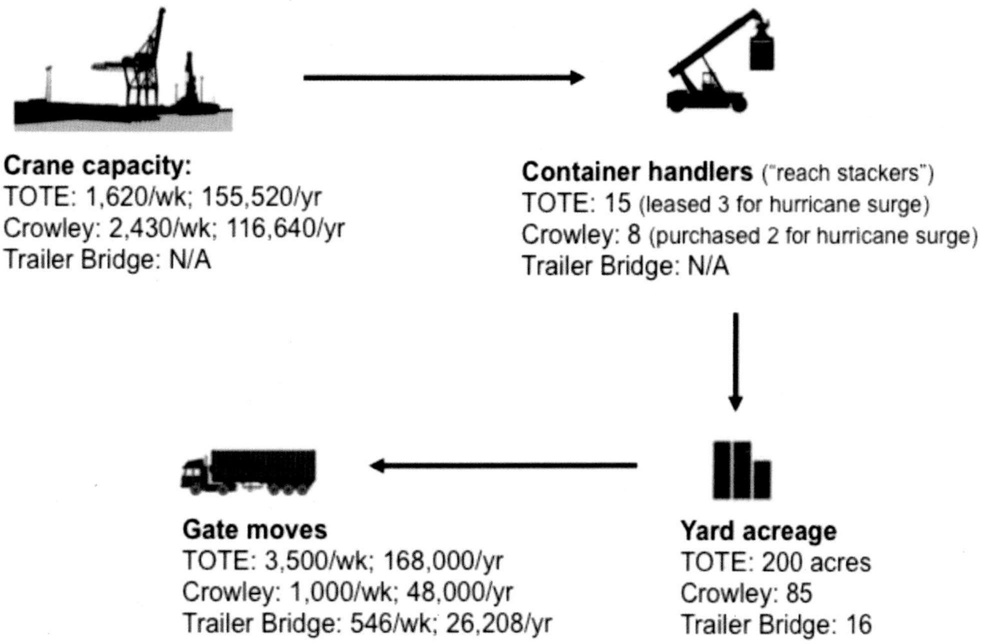

SOURCE: Interviews with TOTE Maritime and Crowley Maritime, Puerto Rico, December 2018. Data for Trailer Bridge are estimated.
NOTE: Year (yr), week (wk), not applicable (N/A).

To estimate the total port throughput capacity in terms of gate moves, we used the number of moves each terminal operator (excluding Trailer Bridge) stated as its normal capacity, as well as its peak capacity per week, and multiplied it by an assumed number of operating weeks per year. The total estimated gate moves per week and year are given in Table 2.5.[18]

[18] To put into perspective the number of gate moves per week, it is possible to calculate the port's implied steady-state utilization. By taking the empirical total TEU imports to San Juan in 2017 (181,244 TEUs) and dividing by the estimated normal number of gate moves per year (242,208 TEUs), the implied utilization is 181,244/242,208 = 0.75. This is in line with most of the port literature that states that terminal yard utilization should be at approximately 70 percent, and overall port utilization should be at less than 80 percent in order to avoid congestion.

Table 2.5. Estimated Throughput Capacity in Number of Truck Gate Moves per Year at the Port of San Juan

Terminal Operator	Operating Weeks per year	Normal: Gate moves per week	Normal: Gate moves per year	Peak: Gate moves per week	Peak: Gate moves per year
Tote Maritime	48	3,500	168,000	5,000	240,000
Crowley Maritime	48	1,000	48,000	1,800	86,400
Trailer Bridge	48	546	26,208	936	44,928
		5,046	242,208	7,736	371,328

SOURCE: Data for TOTE Maritime and Crowley Maritime are from interviews, December 2018. Data for Normal are derived from throughput rates stated by terminal operators to be standard. Data for Peak are derived from throughput rates stated by terminal operators to have been achieved during surge operations several months after Hurricane Maria. Data for Trailer Bridge are estimated.

By looking at the ratio between the peak gate moves achieved after Hurricane Maria and the normal gate moves, it is possible to estimate that the terminal operators at the port can achieve a 371,000/242,000 – 1 = 0.53 or approximately 53-percent increase in throughput.

To estimate how long it would take the terminal operators to increase their capacity from normal to peak levels, we can consider the measures they take. The operators flew in labor from off the island and hired local general laborers, leased or purchased reach-tuggers, leased land from the PRPA, and shifted the way containers are stored in the yard. It may take days to fly in labor and days or weeks to employ new laborers. It may take weeks to acquire new material handling equipment. It may take the terminal operators weeks or a few months to acquire use of leased land. It will take only days for terminal operators to adjust yard storage, as containers typically stay in the yard for less than three days before being picked up by a customer. In total, we estimate that it may take terminal operators several weeks, or between one and two months, to accomplish all these measures and increase their capacity from normal to peak levels.

Bottlenecks at the Port of San Juan Terminals

A link analysis of the container flow across the two largest terminal operators—TOTE Maritime and Crowley Maritime—and interviews with their senior terminal operations leadership reveal that the bottlenecks at the port are a result of insufficient material handling equipment, especially reach stackers, and lack of paved yard space when there are significant surges in demand. The versatility of reach stackers makes them an ideal piece of equipment "for small and medium-sized terminals and for multi-purpose terminals, particularly where there may be a shortage of trained labor for more complex equipment."[19] However, when there is a shortage of reach stackers, moving containers around the terminal becomes increasingly difficult

---

[19] B. Brinkman, "Operations Systems of Container Terminals: A Compendious Overview," in J. Böse, ed., *Handbook of Terminal Planning*, New York: Springer, 2011, pp. 25–39.

and results in greater numbers of containers dwelling at the port. It is estimated that "3 to 4 reach stackers and 4 to 5 tractor trailers are required to keep a ship-to-shore gantry crane fully utilized, with the specific number of tractor trailers depending upon the distance between the berth and stacking area."[20]

Conclusions and Implications

The primary capacity constraint to moving cargo through the Port of San Juan is the infrastructure of berths and quay cranes. Between TOTE Maritime and Crowley Maritime, the two terminal operators have sufficient berths and cranes to increase by at least 50 percent the number of ships they receive. Both operators receive ships on several days of the week, and they perform unloading operations only on the day the ships arrive.

The other capacity constraints in the Port of San Juan are the infrastructure of yard space to store containers, and the resources of labor and reach-tuggers to move cargo. Maritime port terminal capacity is planned under the assumption that demand and cargo movement is fairly stable over time; and as private businesses, the port operators do not incur the expense of planning for surges. Therefore, large and quickly developing surges in demand that are due to unpredicted causes or that are outside the planning of the terminal operators will result in a buildup of containers at the port terminals and a slowdown in port throughput.

By their actions in the months following Hurricane Maria in 2017, the terminal operators exhibited their ability to respond to increasing material flow. In the case of the labor and material handling equipment, the private terminal operators Crowley Maritime and TOTE Maritime were able to respond when it became apparent that they would be unable to meet their demands with the resources they had. They acquired additional reach-tuggers to meet the increased demands experienced in the posthurricane period, and they were able to recruit sufficient additional laborers from Puerto Rico while bringing in some experienced senior staff from their operations in the CONUS. It can be anticipated that the port operators would be able to make similar adjustments to meet increased demand for materials by funded recovery projects. The lead time required to make these adjustments may be a matter of weeks, which would be rapid enough to respond to large increases in demand for logistics capacity owing to recovery projects, if the ramp-up period for the projects is over months (or years).

In the case of additional yard space, the terminal operators do not own the land; they lease it from the PRPA. And it is up to the PRPA to make land or space available for lease, preferably land that is directly adjacent to the current terminal operations so that economies of scale may be realized when it comes to material handling equipment and cargo management and control. Making land available for lease that is off-site or at a distance from current terminal operations

---

[20] Brinkman, 2011, p. 31.

creates an additional management and financial burden on the terminal operators and consumes more resources, especially trucks.

Key actions FEMA or the government of Puerto Rico could take to mitigate future delays in port operations would be to coordinate demands for materials to avoid outsize surges in material flow, and communicate changes in future demand to the port operators; make yard space available; and work through interagency efforts to affect the available supply of trucks and truck drivers and the capacity of customers to receive shipments, to avoid delays in customers picking up materials.

3. Logistics Analysis of the Road Transportation Network

This chapter examines whether the road network in Puerto Rico has enough capacity to accommodate additional use from increased cargo truck shipments delivering materials to funded hurricane recovery projects. This analysis provides background on key network assets, particularly the strategic highway network within the island, and assesses potential difficulties with first and last mile transportation, travel speeds, bridge conditions, and the availability of trucks and truck drivers.

Overview of Roads in Puerto Rico

This section includes a summary description of the road infrastructure network in Puerto Rico, its status before and after Hurricanes Maria and Irma. A detailed overview is available in other research performed by HSOAC.[1]

Key Assets

Consisting of approximately 16,500 miles of roadway on an island of 5,300 square miles, Puerto Rico's road network is among the densest in the United States. The network also features over 2,000 bridges and two tunnels.

Roads are characterized in a few ways, such as by the entity responsible for managing them, by whether they receive federal funding, by urban or rural location, or by functional classification (interstate vs. local).[2] Table 3.1 summarizes road assets in Puerto Rico. About two-thirds of the network is owned by the municipalities, which are responsible for its maintenance but not necessarily its design, construction, or any major overhaul. The Puerto Rico Department of Transportation, Departamento de Transportación y Obras Publicias (DTOP), owns the remaining fraction of the network; this includes 3,500 miles of federal-aid roads that contain all the road segments that compose the National Highway System in Puerto Rico.[3] Federal-aid roads receive support that is administered by the Federal Highway Administration (FHWA).

[1] RAND Corporation, Spring 2019.

[2] RAND Corporation, Spring 2019.

[3] Approximately 30 miles of roads are owned and operated by other federal agencies. These roads are primarily on national lands, such as El Yunque, a national forest owned by the National Forest Service, and in several wildlife refuges, owned by the U.S. Fish and Wildlife Service.

Table 3.1. Rural and Urban Roads in Centerline Miles by Ownership and Functional Class (2014)

	Total number of miles: 16,650			
	Rural total: 3,100		Urban total: 13,550	
By ownership:	**DTOP**	**Municipalities**	**DTOP**	**Municipalities**
Total:	**1,025**	**2,060**	**3,560**	**10,010**
Federal-aid	545	0	2,710	220
Non-federal-aid	480	2,060	850	9,790
By functional class:				
Interstates	40		255	
Other freeways and expressways	0		50	
Other principal arterial	45		380	
Minor arterial	225		930	
Major collector	220		1120	
Minor collector	240		0	
Local roads	2,300		11,385	

SOURCES: RAND Corporation, 2019; Ownership: FHWA, *Highway Performance Monitoring System*, Tables HM-14 and HM-10, 2018; Functional class: FHWA, Table HM-20, 2018.
NOTE: Numbers are rounded to the nearest 5. Totals are slightly inconsistent between different tables in the Highway Performance Monitoring System (HPMS). Puerto Rico's only local government entities are municipalities, which serve both city and county functions.

Of interest is the island's strategic highway network, which is shown in Figure 3.1. The strategic highway network consists of preidentified roads that are deemed essential to the U.S. Department of Defense's domestic operations for activities such as emergency mobilization and peacetime movement of heavy armor, fuel, ammunition, repair parts, food, and other commodities to support U.S. military operations. Moreover, all these roads are interstates on the island and major transisland thoroughfares that are used daily by residents. Table 3.2 summarizes various design characteristics of the highways and usage prior to the hurricanes in 2016.

Figure 3.1. Strategic Highway Network in Puerto Rico

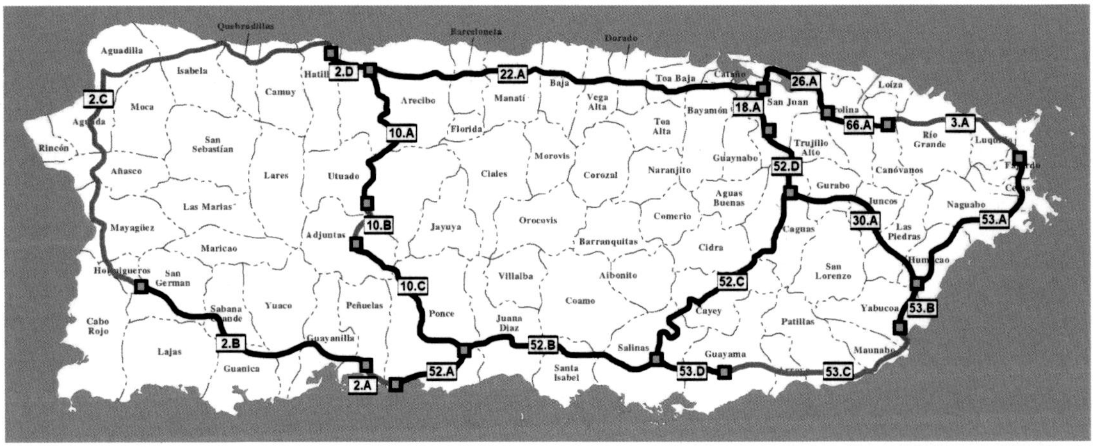

NOTE: Red corresponds to sections that are not completed or require rehabilitation.

Table 3.2. Characteristics of Strategic Highway Network

Route	Segment	Distance (miles)	Vehicle Miles Traveled	Maximum Lanes[b]	Minimum Lanes[b]	Mode Lanes[b,c]
PR-2	02.A	7.1	291,693	3	2	2
PR-2	02.B	25.0	805,852	2	2	2
PR-2	02.C	55.7	2,085,136	3	2	2
PR-2	02.D	4.6	117,431	2	2	2
PR-3	03.A	14.4	506,066	3	2	2
PR-10	10.A	21.8	223,021	3	1	3
PR-10[a]	10.B	3.4	NA	NA	NA	NA
PR-10	10.C	17.2	204,732	3	1	2
PR-18	18.A	3.7	769,162	5	5	5
PR-22	22.A	50.3	3,550,005	5	2	2
PR-26	26.A	8.3	808,211	4	2	4
PR-30	30.A	19.1	1,326,868	4	2	2
PR-52	52.A	6.5	279,853	2	2	2
PR-52	52.B	22.9	852,204	2	2	2
PR-52	52.C	28.1	1,475,026	3	2	2
PR-52	52.D	9.8	1,123,812	5	3	3
PR-53	53.A	21.0	380,950	2	2	2
PR-53	53.B	11.2	132,240	2	2	2
PR-53	53.C	19.9	83,450	2	1	2
PR-53	53.D	6.3	123,541	2	2	2
PR-66	66.A	12.2	364,052	2	2	2

SOURCE: Data from DTOP, "General Design Criteria," chapter 1 in *Design Manual*, Puerto Rico Highway and Transportation Authority, 1979.
NOTE: Highway segments correspond to segments depicted in Figure 3.1.
Not available (NA).
[a] Segment 10.B of PR-10 is not completed.
[b] Number of lanes in the peak direction.
[c] Mode number of lanes calculated using the mode of road subsegments in DTOP data.

Since any transisland shipping and transportation will likely use the strategic highway network for most of its transit distance, this particular network will be the focus of all road-related transportation logistics analyzed in this report; however, "first" and "last" mile transportation using local roads that are off this network is discussed.

Physical Conditions of Assets

Overall, major roads in Puerto Rico, including those off the strategic network, were in fair condition prior to Hurricane Maria (on a scale of good/fair/poor).[4] The condition of the pavement is based on its roughness, the extent of cracking and road faulting, and the depth of ruts. More extensive data are available for federal-aid roads, which include the strategic highways. Figure 3.2 depicts the geographic locations of the sections of federal-aid roads that

[4] RAND Corporation, Spring 2019.

are in good (green), fair (black), and poor (red) condition prior to the hurricanes. The condition of these roads since the hurricane remains dynamic, as repairs and maintenance are ongoing.

Figure 3.2. Map of Pavement Conditions on Federal-Aid Roads in Puerto Rico

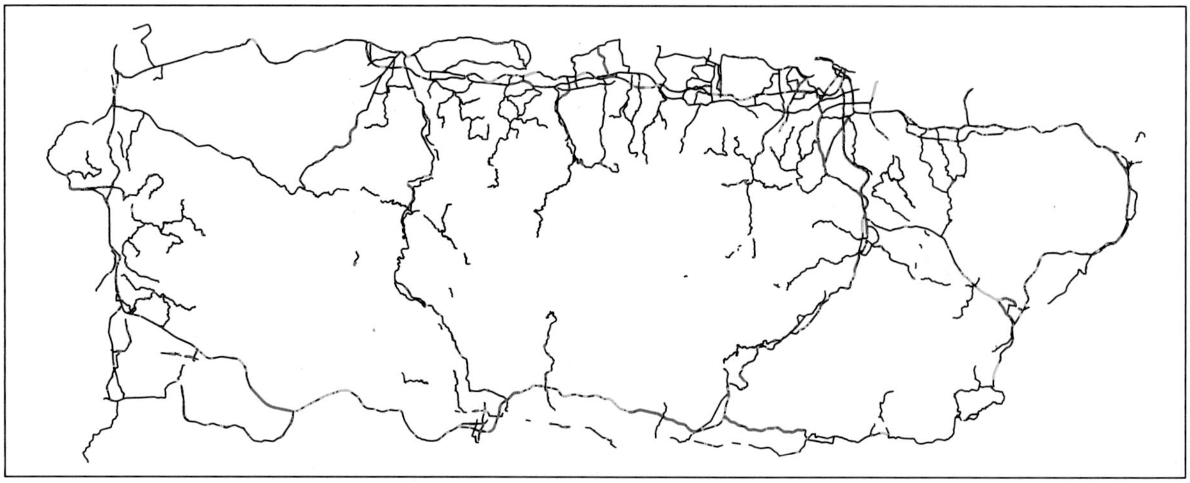

SOURCE: RAND Corporation, 2019.
NOTE: Good condition (green); fair condition (black); poor condition (red).

In 2017, FHWA assessed the conditions of the bridges in the National Bridge Inventory (NBI) and categorized them as either "structurally deficient" or not, as well as being in a "good," "fair," or "poor" condition.[5] Of the 2,325 bridges in the NBI, 301 were structurally deficient (13 percent).[6] Additionally, 446 (19 percent), 1,608 (69 percent), and 271 (12 percent) bridges were assessed as being in good, fair, or poor condition, respectively.[7]

The Recovery Effort

As part of the Puerto Rico disaster recovery program coordinated by FEMA after Hurricane Maria (FEMA-4339-DR-PR), the Commonwealth of Puerto Rico has elected to participate in "alternative procedures" for all large project funding for Public Assistance categories C–G, pursuant to Section 428 of the Stafford Act.[8] HSOAC is providing analyses and independent reviews of projects funded with Public Assistance.

---

[5] RAND Corporation, Spring 2019.

[6] RAND Corporation, Spring 2019.

[7] RAND Corporation, Spring 2019.

[8] 42 U.S.C. § 5121.

HSOAC analyses[9] have investigated the economic impact of the hurricanes and subsequent recovery package. The most recent draft plan estimates that total public assistance expenditures will be $132 billion over the following decade, yielding over $10 billion annually in recovery spending (HSOAC projects the effect if funds are spent at varied rates throughout the years, ranging from a rate of $1 billion to $25 billion per year). Detailed economic analyses of the COAs indicate that about one-half of annual public assistance expenditures will go toward the construction sector, with the remainder going toward the administrative, company management, and educational sectors.[10] One conclusion of this analysis is that approximately 2,300 additional truck drivers will be needed, a 29-percent increase from the approximate 8,000 employed in 2017 (the increase would be up to 5,800 additional truck drivers if spending is at a rate of $25 billion per year).

The recovery effort will undoubtedly induce additional demand on the road network and its resources. It is unclear at what pace the demand for trucking services will increase. At the time of this report, requests for funding are only beginning to arrive at FEMA. Steps to follow include awarding of funds and awarding contracts. To meet the demands of the economy, the labor market must adjust (with or without support from government agencies) to increase prices and attract truck drivers (wages in Puerto Rico for this work are about half of what they would be in the CONUS).[11] Truck drivers may be new to the occupation and thus require training and licensing. It takes about seven to nine weeks to earn a commercial driver's license by attending a commercial trucking school full time.[12] Or truck drivers may come from the CONUS. Trucks will also have to be imported to Puerto Rico. The whole of the United States is facing a shortage of truck drivers.

Additional burden on the network may manifest through extended travel times, diminished travel speeds, congestion, and reduced throughput of island trucking. We conducted several analyses to determine whether the network has enough capacity to absorb this demand. Our analyses consider several factors in making this determination:

1. Ease of first and last mile road transportation
2. Current travel times and travel speeds on the highway network at different times of the day
3. Structural or clearance issues pending for bridges on the highway network
4. Congestion of the highway network and maximum allowable trucking throughput before significant congestion is likely to occur.

---

[9] RAND Corporation, Spring 2019.

[10] RAND Corporation, Spring 2019.

[11] RAND Corporation, Spring 2019.

[12] J. F. Morgan et al., "On the Training and Testing of Entry-Level Commercial Motor Vehicle Drivers," *Accident Analysis & Prevention*, Vol. 43, No. 4, 2011, pp. 1400–1407.

Methods

This section describes the methods used in the research.

First and Last Mile Transportation

As discussed in other sections of this report, the Port of San Juan is the likely transshipment point for all seaborne freight entering Puerto Rico. The port features three terminals: Isla Grande, Puerto de Tierra, and Puerto Nuevo—all of which are in densely populated areas of San Juan. The first miles of road transportation (for destinations outside San Juan) will occur after trucks exit the port terminals and join the highway network. The last miles will occur after exiting the highway network and utilizing local roads to reach destinations.

To assess the first miles traveled by trucks, the research team followed trucks exiting the Port of San Juan in December 2018 and drove the routes from each of the port terminals to the nearest highway network entrance. The research team noted the number of lanes, lane width, at-grade intersections, traffic signals, and other factors that could impede traffic.

For assessment of the last miles, the research team selected one town among the four towns of Lares, Orocovis, Benitez, and Rosa Sanchez. These four towns are near the geographic centroids of the interior regions of the highway network as shown in Figure 3.1. Both Lares and Orocovis are at high elevations that necessitate the use of winding, often single-lane, local roads in mountainous terrain (up to 1,300 ft), with the former being closer to an uncompleted section of the strategic highway network (PR-10). We therefore selected the town of Lares as a destination point from the Port of San Juan. The research team examined the feasibility of trucks using these roads and having sufficiently sized staging areas to unload the freight.

Travel Speeds and Times on Highway Network

We estimate current travel speeds and travel times using the proprietary Google Maps application programming interface (API)[13] and Python 3.6. The API was queried hourly for each highway segment from Monday, December 10, 2018, 8:00 a.m., until Monday, December 17, 7:00 a.m.[14] These data were analyzed to identify the best times of day for additional truck shipments on each segment of the highway network.

---

[13] Google, "Distance Maps API," undated.

[14] The Google API offers three estimates of travel duration: best guess, optimistic, and pessimistic. Best guess is based on both average historical traffic conditions and live traffic. The optimistic guess is given as the duration shorter than the actual travel time on most days. The pessimistic guess is given as the duration longer than the actual travel time on most days, though occasional days with particularly bad traffic conditions may exceed this value. We used the pessimistic guess in all of the analyses.

Bridge Conditions

Data from 2017 on bridges along segments of the highway net are available from the NBI.[15] We reviewed the bridge data to assess, along each highway segment, bridge conditions (good, fair, poor), minimum vertical clearance, and structural evaluation code (SEC).

Bridges in poor condition are likely to require servicing and create additional delays. Moreover, FHWA recommends at least a 4.3-meter minimum vertical clearance for trucks. Bridges with significantly less clearance can result in delays, as vehicles may have to be rerouted or a smaller class thereof must be used. The SEC characterizes the load-bearing capability of the bridge. The rating ranges from 0 to 9 and depends on the average daily traffic (i.e., traffic volume utilizing the bridge) and the number of metric tons the bridge can sustain for a long period (inventory rating).[16] Bridges with ratings less than 4 require either corrective action or replacement.

Congestion and Trucking Throughput

This subsection presents a model to determine whether additional demand, measured by the number of additional trucks using the network, can indeed be absorbed by the highway network without creating excessive congestion.

Level of Service

Congestion is measured using level of service (LOS). It is a rating ranging from A to F that indicates the level of congestion and ease of traffic flow. LOS may be calculated from the ratio of traffic volume to highway capacity for a given free-flow speed (FFS).[17] Table 3.3 summarizes the different ratings and corresponding volume-to-capacity ranges. LOS A indicates free flow, LOS B–D indicate reasonable speeds with increasing risk of blockages, and LOS E–F indicate that the segment is unstable or approaching instability.

---

[15] FHWA, "National Bridge Inventory," 2017.

[16] FHWA, *Recording and Coding Guide for the Structure Inventory and Appraisal of the Nation's Bridges*, Report FHWA-PD-96-001, Washington, D.C., 1995.

[17] Transportation Research Board, *Highway Capacity Manual: HCM 2010*. Transportation Research Board, Washington, D.C., 2010.

Table 3.3. LOS

LOS	Description	Volume-to-Capacity Range at FFS of 55 mph[a]	Volume-to-Capacity at FFSs of 60–64 mph[a]
A	Free-flow operation	0.00–0.27	0.00–0.29
B	Reasonably free flow Ability to maneuver is only slightly restricted Effects of minor incidents still easily absorbed	0.27–0.44	0.29–0.47
C	Speeds at or near FFS Freedom to maneuver is noticeably restricted Queues may form behind any significant blockage	0.44–0.64	0.47–0.68
D	Speeds decline slightly with increasing flows Density increases more quickly Freedom to maneuver is more noticeably limited Minor incidents create queuing	0.64–0.85	0.68–0.88
E	Operation near or at capacity No usable gaps in the traffic stream Operations extremely volatile Any disruption causes queuing	0.85–1.00	0.88–1.00
F	Unstable Breakdown in flow Queues form behind breakdown points Demand > capacity	≥ 1.00	≥ 1.00

[a] Corresponds to assumed FFS.
Miles per hour (mph).

Highway Capacity

Calculation of LOS relies on the calculation of traffic volumes and capacities for each of the highway segments. Capacity is estimated using the FHWA Simplified Highway Capacity Calculation Method for the HPMS.[18] There are distinct models for the different types of highways on the island's highway network.

Interstates and limited-access freeways are the most common type of highway on the network. For these highways, capacity is calculated as follows:

$$Capacity = \frac{Lanes \cdot (2200 + 10\,(\min(70, FFS) - 50))}{1 + HV},$$

where $Lanes$ is the number of lanes in the peak direction, FFS is the assumed free-flow speed, and HV is the fraction of traffic consisting of trucks and heavy vehicles. The other type of highway is a multilane highway (which might not be limited access or built to interstate specifications), for which capacity is estimated using the following equation:

[18] R. Margiotta and S. Washburn, *Simplified Highway Capacity Calculation Method for the Highway Performance Monitoring System*, Report for Federal Highway Administration, PL-18-003, Washington, D.C.: Federal Highway Administration, October 2017; FHWA, 2018; Transportation Research Board, 2010.

$$Capacity = Base\ Capacity \cdot f_{HV} \cdot Lanes,$$

where

$$Base\ Capacity = 1000 + 20 \cdot FFS; for\ FFS \leq 60; 2{,}200\ otherwise,$$

$$f_{HV} = \frac{1}{(1 + HV \cdot ET)}.$$

ET is an adjustment factor for terrain, and *FFS*, *HV*, and *Lanes* (peak) are defined as before.

Higher fractions of heavy trucks and vehicles heighten the risk of congestion. DTOP design criteria assume that *HV* ranges from 0.0 to 0.18 for rural highways,[19] which typically have a higher fraction of trucks and heavy vehicles than urban highways. We assume that the initial fraction of trucks and heavy vehicles is 0.18, which is a conservative assumption as a higher fraction reduces the available capacity. This fraction will increase as additional trucks from the recovery operations are added, and other light purpose vehicles are not added to the roadways in proportion.

FFS, which differs from observed speed, is the assumed speed a vehicle would travel in low-volume conditions. *FFS* depends on an assumed base speed, with adjustments for lane width and lateral clearance (right shoulder width). Interstates and freeways have a standard base speed of 75.4 mph. According to the 2016 HPMS data for Puerto Rico, lane widths of the highways range from 8 to 12 ft with an average of 11 ft per lane. For the analysis, we conservatively assumed that lane widths are narrower than average (10 ft) and that lateral clearances are limited. According to recommended FHWA calculations,[20] the adjusted *FFS* is 63.4 mph for interstates and freeways; for highways that are neither freeways nor interstates, we assume *FFS* is significantly less than 60.0 mph when calculating capacity.

Traffic Volume

There are several methods to calculate traffic volume. A data-driven approach employs a commonly obtained measurement of traffic volume known as the average annual daily traffic (AADT).[21] AADT measures daily traffic volume over a given road segment; however, this volume will not be distributed uniformly over the day.

Of interest is the peak or design hourly volume, which is the defined as the thirtieth worst hourly volume in a year. In practice, this quantity is estimated from AADT using two factors: the *K* factor and the *D* factor. The *K* factor is the proportion of AADT that represents traffic during the peak hour in either direction. The *D* factor is the proportion of peak traffic that is traveling in

---

[19] DTOP, Puerto Rico Highway and Transportation Authority, 2016.

[20] FHWA, 2018.

[21] AADT is the total annual number of vehicles that traveled on a given highway segment (here, in either direction) divided by the number of travel days in the year.

the peak direction. DTOP design criteria assume that *K* ranges from 0.07 to 0.15 and that the HPMS default value for the *D* factor is 0.55.[22] We assume that the *K* factor is 0.15 (the most conservative value in DTOP's range) and that the *D* factor is 0.55.

Data and Calculations of Level of Service at Peak Hour

The 2016 capacity and volume data for highway segments were obtained from DTOP.[23] The dataset includes data for smaller segments of each highway segment—which we hereafter refer to as subsegments. Under the foregoing assumptions, we calculated LOS during peak hour for each subsegment.

Trucking Throughput

If the recovery effort increases the number of trucks using a highway segment, then in addition to the increased traffic volume, the capacity of the highway segment will diminish because of the rise in the fraction of heavy vehicles. The volume-to-capacity ratio will increase and result in further congestion and possibly a worse LOS.

We calculated the maximum number of additional trucks (per hour) that can use a given highway segment before the LOS of any subsegment deteriorates to LOS E or worse. These trucks use the network in addition to other users, and the observed LOS depends on whether this additional use occurs when volume is already at peak, near-peak, or off-peak. Since additional use at peak would not be recommended, we performed this calculation under two scenarios: (1) 70 percent of peak volume (near-peak) and (2) 40 percent of peak volume (off-peak). This calculation was performed using a numerical root-finding algorithm in Microsoft® Excel.

Results

First and Last Miles

First Miles

The research team did not identify any issues with transportation of freight leaving the Port of San Juan, and besides minor delays owing to local traffic conditions in San Juan, the team did not identify any major issues entering the highway network.[24] From the Isla Grande terminal, a departing truck would move a short distance from Calle Lindbergh to PR-35 or PR-16 and then proceed to either PR-26 or PR-22 via PR 1-S—up to 2.5 miles on a signalized two-lane road with

---

[22] DTOP, Puerto Rico Highway and Transportation Authority, 2016; FHWA, 2018.

[23] DTOP, Puerto Rico Highway and Transportation Authority, 2016.

[24] The research team watched trucks leave the Port of San Juan and join the highway network, in daylight hours and clear weather. The roads allowed two trucks to drive in parallel and enter the highway without traffic delay. This analysis was not inclusive of all the highway entrances or frontage roads in the San Juan area.

a minimum of five at-grade intersections before an on-ramp to the freeway. These routes pass the San Juan convention center and are subject to minor inconveniences. From the Puerta de Tierra terminal in Old San Juan, a truck would drive east on Calle Marina and proceed toward PR-26 or PR-22 via PR 1-S along a two-lane signalized road with at least three signalized intersections and a two-lane bridge (one of the two bridges into San Juan in the area) and passing a fire station (up to three miles). From the Puerto Nuevo terminal, which is serviced by an interchange with PR-2, a truck can enter the freeway directly and travel to PR-22 (less than two miles).

Analysis of Google Maps data for these routes indicates that in good conditions trucks can enter the highway network in less than 10 minutes, but in peak conditions, this make take up to 25 minutes for routes departing Old San Juan. However, once the truck enters the highway, it is still subject to traffic conditions in San Juan, which may be heavily congested during peak hours.

Last Miles

While San Juan is the presumed point of origin for the freight, the research team noted some potential difficulties with sending heavy trucks to interior towns such as Lares. For example, one of the most accessible routes to this town from the west involves traveling single-lane, winding, nonsignalized roads at steeply increasing or decreasing elevations (PR-111). The research team observed cases where in order to allow vehicles from opposite directions to pass, vehicles had to pull over and yield to oncoming traffic. On the routes the team traveled, there was limited to no shoulder space for parking heavy trucks, although potential staging areas were scattered intermittently near the roadway and being used as such. The team also witnessed medium and light trucks successfully navigating these roads, but no heavy trucks. Freight arriving to such destinations will have to use lighter trucks in San Juan or transfer material from heavy trucks to lighter truckers nearer to the destination, potentially adding some delay, inconvenience, and cost.

Travel Speeds and Fastest Times of Day to Travel

Table 3.4 presents current weekday travel speeds for highway segments at peak (morning and afternoon rush), midday (11:00 a.m.–3:00 p.m.), and nondaytime hours. Travel on Puerto Rico's roads, especially outbound from San Juan, is mostly constrained during peak hours. Figure 3.3 presents the hours in a typical weekday where speeds are at 70 percent of their maximum or higher. For example, trucks departing from San Juan toward Arecibo would travel fastest along PR-22 West if departing between 8:00 a.m. and 3:00 p.m. or between 7:00 p.m. and 4:00 a.m.

Table 3.4. Estimated Weekday Average Travel Speeds on Strategic Highway Network (mph)

Route	Segment	Peak	Midday (11:00 a.m.–3:00 p.m.)	Nondaytime
PR-2	02.A	33	36	49
PR-2	02.B	49	52	60
PR-2	02.C	17	21	49
PR-2	02.D	14	16	31
PR-3	03.A	19	22	43
PR-10	10.A	36	39	44
PR-10[a]	10.B	19	20	23
PR-10	10.C	38	41	48
PR-18	18.A	12	24	45
PR-22	22.A	23	43	58
PR-26	26.A	15	34	48
PR-30	30.A	29	41	58
PR-52	52.A	38	43	51
PR-52	52.B	34	46	62
PR-52	52.C	33	42	54
PR-52	52.D	14	37	55
PR-53	53.A	43	46	53
PR-53	53.B	45	47	55
PR-53	53.C	23	26	31
PR-53	53.D	47	50	57
PR-66	66.A	45	49	59

SOURCE: Data from Google Maps.
NOTES: Highway segments correspond to segments depicted in Figure 3.1.
[a] Segment 10.B of PR-10 is not completed. Travel speeds are shown for best detour.

Figure 3.3. Times of Weekday with the Fastest Travel Speeds

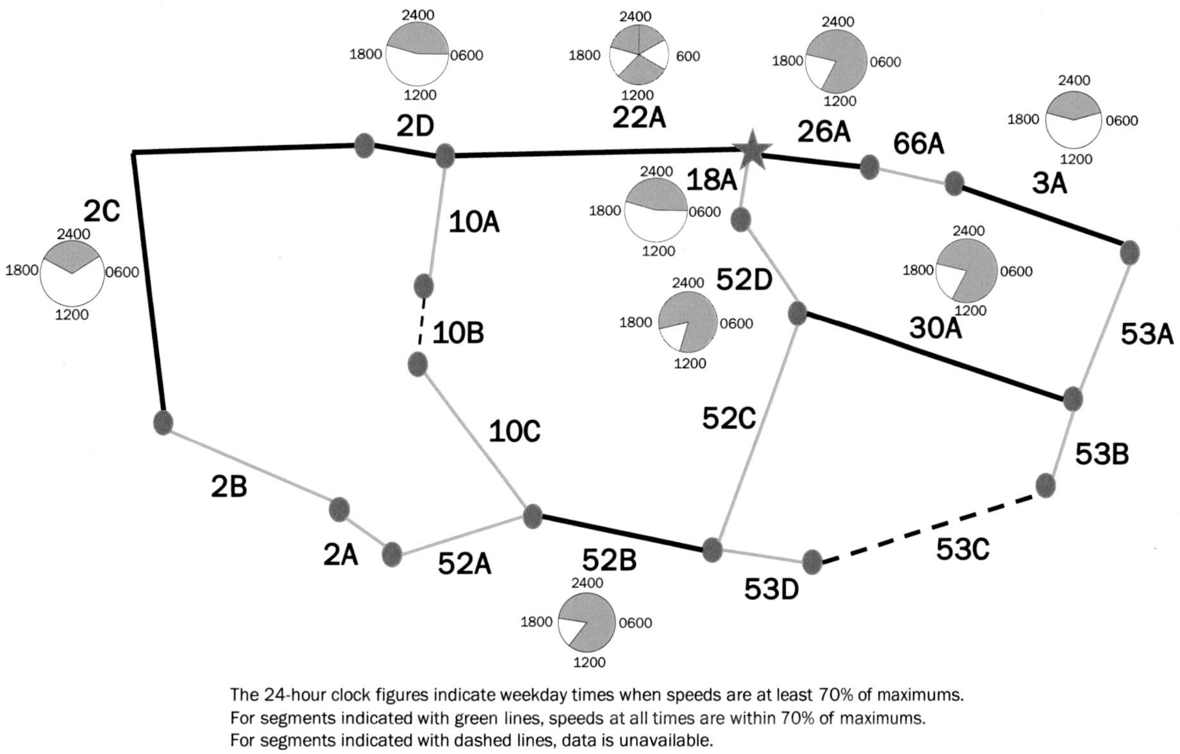

SOURCE: Data from Google Maps.
NOTE: Highway segments correspond to segments depicted in Figure 3.1.

Bridge Conditions

Figure 3.4 summarizes the conditions of bridges on the highway network. Most structures are in fair condition (557/790, 71 percent), followed by good condition (176/790, 22 percent), and poor condition (57/790, 7 percent). PR-18 and PR-52 (segment 52-A west of Ponce) have the highest share of poor structures (about 30 percent). Bridges in poor condition are more likely to be serviced sooner and cause potential disruptions and slowdowns.

Figure 3.4. Conditions of Bridges on Highway Network

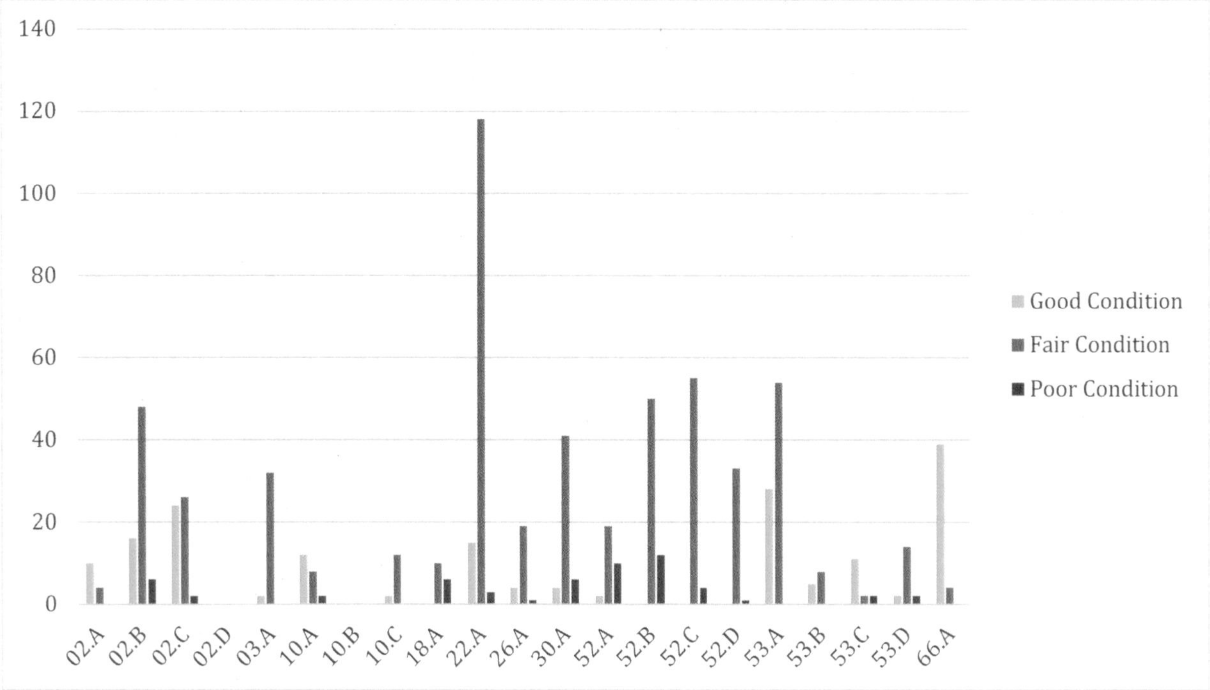

NOTE: Highway segments correspond to segments depicted in Figure 3.1. PR-2 segment 2D has no bridges, and PR-10 segment 10B is not completed. We count as a bridge each bridge structure in one direction. For example, an east-west highway with one bridge structure would count as two bridges, one in the east direction and one in the west direction. The terms "good" (G), "fair" (F), and "poor" (P) are defined in accordance with the Pavement and Bridge Condition Performance Measures final rule, published in January 2017. Bridge condition is determined by the lowest rating of NBI condition ratings for Item 58 (Deck), Item 59 (Superstructure), Item 60 (Substructure), or Item 62 (Culvert). If the lowest rating is greater than or equal to 7, the bridge is classified as good; if it is less than or equal to 4, it is classified as poor. Bridges rated 5 or 6 are classified as fair. FHWA, "Tables of Frequently Requested NBI Information," undated.

Two bridges with less than 4.3-meter vertical clearance were identified: (1) on PR-22, 3 km west of Barceloneta (4.26 m) and (2) on PR-53 (segment 53-D), 2.5 km west of Manubo.[25] The former bridge is in poor condition and the latter is in good condition.

Figure 3.5 summarizes the number of bridges with an SEC of 3 or less (i.e., requiring corrective action, replacement/closure). Eighteen bridges with an SEC of 3 were identified, and no bridges had an SEC of less than 3. These bridges will require corrective action and are potentially disruptive to future traffic patterns. Moreover, assuming inventory ratings do not decrease, SECs for all remaining bridges on the network will not change because of the increases in average daily traffic from the recovery stimulus. Figure 3.6 depicts the locations of bridges in poor condition or with an SEC of 3 or less.

---

[25] The data also contained two bridges on PR-22 with unknown vertical clearance.

Figure 3.5. Bridges with an SEC of 3 or Less on the Highway Network

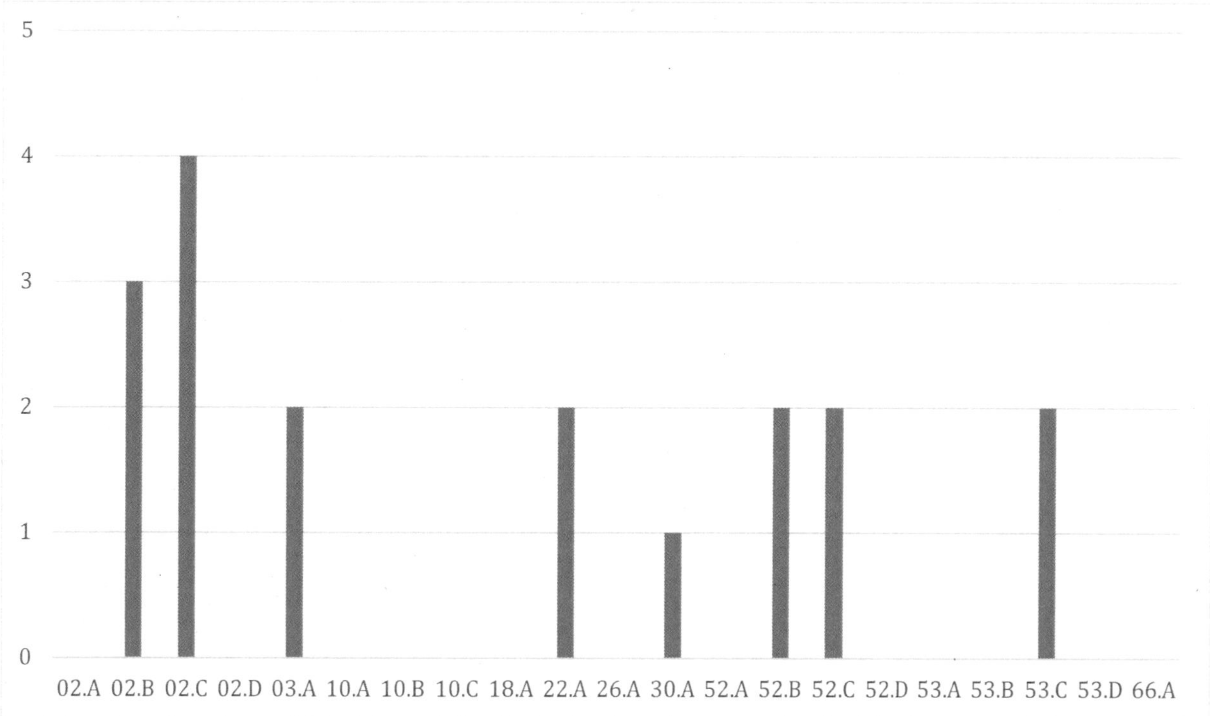

NOTE: Highway segments correspond to segments depicted in Figure 3.1. SEC ratings for all reported bridges were 3 and not 2 or 0. We count as a bridge a bridge structure in one direction. For example, an east-west highway with one bridge structure would count as two bridges, one in the east direction and one in the west direction. The terms "good" (G), "fair" (F), and "poor" (P) are defined in accordance with the Pavement and Bridge Condition Performance Measures final rule, published in January 2017. Bridge condition is determined by the lowest rating of NBI condition ratings for Item 58 (Deck), Item 59 (Superstructure), Item 60 (Substructure), or Item 62 (Culvert). If the lowest rating is greater than or equal to 7, the bridge is classified as good; if it is less than or equal to 4, it is classified as poor. Bridges rated 5 or 6 are classified as fair. FHWA, undated.

Figure 3.6. Locations of Bridges in Poor Condition or with an SEC of 3 or Less on the Highway Network

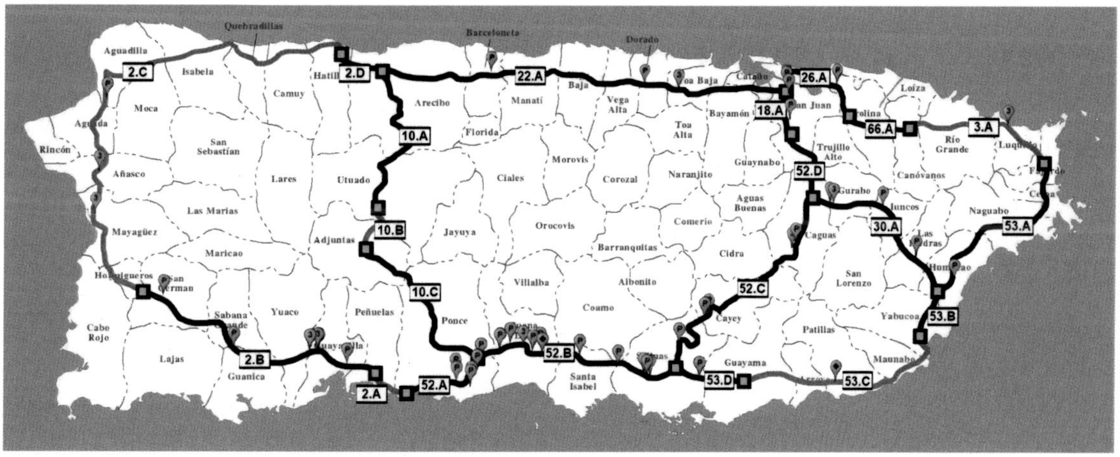

NOTE: Value of "P" indicates bridge structure in poor condition, "3" indicates an SEC of 3, and a diamond indicates both.

Level of Service and Trucking Throughput

Figure 3.7 depicts LOS for segments of the highway network at peak volume. Highways servicing San Juan (PR-22, PR-18, PR-52, and PR-26) and Ponce (PR-52 and PR-10) are heavily congested at peak hours and possess sections of road with LOS F. Other slowdowns occur at interchanges or when otherwise-moving highways suddenly enter relatively populated areas, such as Carrizales, Juana Diaz, Mayaguez, and Playa Fortuna.

Figure 3.7. LOS on Highway Network at Peak

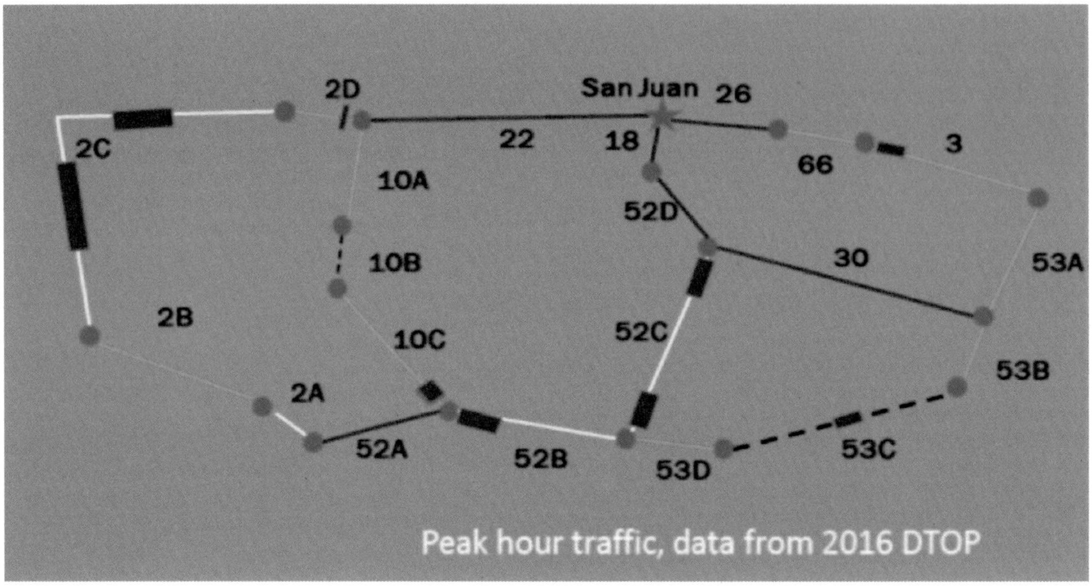

SOURCE: DTOP, Puerto Rico Highway and Transportation Authority, 2016.
NOTE: Highway segments correspond to segments depicted in Figure 3.1. Red: LOS F, unstable breakdown in flow; queues form behind breakdown points. Yellow: LOS E, operation near or at capacity; no usable gaps in the traffic stream; operations extremely volatile; any disruption causes queuing. Green: LOS A–D free flow but with speeds declining slightly with increasing flows. Segment PR-10B is not complete, and data were not available for all subsegments of segment PR-53C.

Table 3.5 and Figure 3.8 summarize the maximum number of trucks per hour a highway segment can absorb before a section of it enters LOS E or worse at 40 percent (off-peak) or 70 percent (near-peak) of peak volume. Near-peak corresponds roughly to daytime nonrush hours and off-peak to nighttime hours. Highways near San Juan are most constrained in the number of trucks they can absorb per hour, particularly on highways PR-18, PR-22, PR-30, and PR-52 (segment 52-D). At near-peak, these highways will always be at risk of slowdown regardless of additional trucks entering the highway. Notably, even at off-peak, outbound traffic from San Juan using PR-18, PR-22, and PR-52 is constrained to 134, 361, or 312 additional trucks per hour, respectively, before risk of congestion. Eastbound traffic using PR-30 is limited to less than an additional 100 trucks per hour according to the model.

Table 3.5. Maximum Number of Trucks (per Hour) Before Highway Segment Enters LOS E or Worse

Route	Segment	Near-Peak (70% Peak Volume)	Off-Peak (40% Peak Volume)
PR-2	02.A	644	1,821
PR-2	02.B	1,119	2,099
PR-2	02.C	365	1,658
PR-2	02.D	897	1,948
PR-3	03.A	644	1,821
PR-10	10.A	1,153	1,387
PR-10	10.B[a]	–	–
PR-10	10.C	1,040	1,331
PR-18	18.A	0[c]	134
PR-22	22.A	0[c]	361
PR-26	26.A	0[c]	1,169
PR-30	30.A	0[c]	64
PR-52	52.A	0[c]	1,323
PR-52	52.B	229	1,578
PR-52	52.C	0[c]	1,304
PR-52	52.D	0[c]	312
PR-53	53.A	1,812	2,505
PR-53	53.B	1,905	2,559
PR-53	53.C[b]	–	–
PR-53	53.D	2,091	2,668
PR-66	66.A	1,741	2,463

NOTE: Highway segments correspond to segments depicted in Figure 3.1.
[a] Segment 10.B of PR-10 is not completed.
[b] Insufficient data.
[c] Segment already begins with section in LOS E or worse at assumed volume.

Figure 3.8. Maximum Number of Trucks (per Hour) Before Highway Segment Enters LOS E or Worse (Near-Peak/Off-Peak)

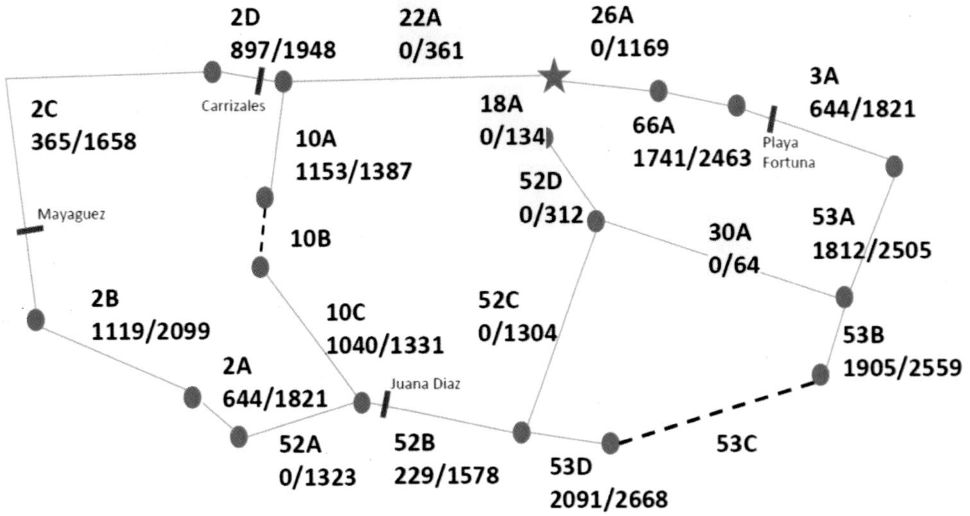

NOTE: Highway segments correspond to segments depicted in Figure 3.1. Near-peak corresponds to 70 percent of peak volume. Off-peak corresponds to 40 percent of peak volume. Value of 0 indicates segment contains section in LOS E or worse at assumed volume. Segment 10.B of PR-10 is not completed. Insufficient data for Segment 53.C of PR-53.

The analysis indicates that outbound traffic from San Juan (eastbound using PR-26 and west/southbound using PR-18, PR-22, PR-30, or PR-52) may be the most constrained across the strategic distribution network, if there is an increase in traffic due to cargo arriving for recovery projects. Using the estimated increase in trucks carrying cargo out of the port for recovery projects, and recent traffic data, we can project what the effect would be of the increase in vehicles on the road.

Taking a look at the pattern of trucks leaving the port, using AADT data, we estimate that 63 percent of the trucks would enter the highways heading westbound and southbound, and 27 percent of the trucks would head eastbound. If 2,300 additional trucks (representing the increase in heavy vehicle use in Puerto Rico resulting from the recovery projects) were released near to peak times, approximately 1,449 trucks (0.63 × 2,300) would overwhelm westbound and southbound routes during near-peak or off-peak hours (as an increase only of 100–400 trucks per hour on those routes would overwhelm their capacity at those times). The remaining 621 (0.27 × 2,300) trucks heading eastbound via PR-26 could not be absorbed near-peak but could be absorbed off-peak as sufficient remaining capacity is available. Highways outside the vicinity of San Juan can accommodate over 1,300 trucks per hour off-peak and should be able to accommodate the majority of this traffic afterward.

State of the Trucking Industry in Puerto Rico and the United States

This section describes the current state of the truck driver occupation in Puerto Rico and the overall challenge to hire truck drivers in the United States.

Makeup of the Trucking Occupation in Puerto Rico

A number of data sources provide information on the truck driver occupation and participation of firms in trucking. The data converge to indicate there are approximately 8,000 truck drivers working in Puerto Rico. Many of these individuals work in small businesses, employing five or fewer people. This is particularly true of those who work transporting cargo from ports onward to locations in Puerto Rico. Of the larger firms employing truck drivers, many of them are for businesses not involved in the seaborne supply chain.

U.S. Census County Business Patterns 2016

The U.S. census lists 7,728 individuals working in trucking-related businesses, with 1,216 establishments (businesses) in Puerto Rico. Most of the truck drivers (95 percent) work at establishments with fewer than five employees (Figure 3.9).[26]

Figure 3.9. Number of Employees in Trucking Firms in Puerto Rico

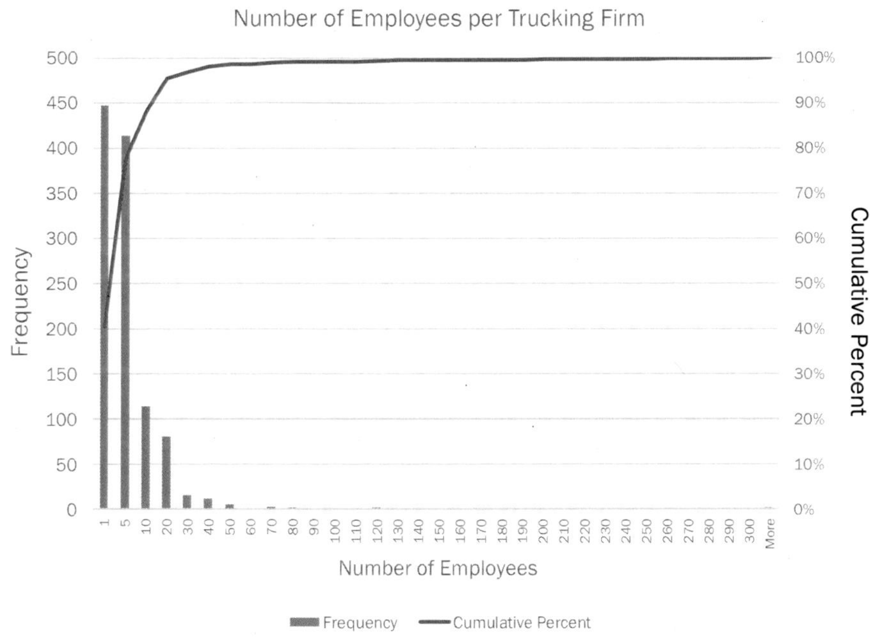

SOURCE: U.S. Census Bureau, "County Business Patterns: 2016," webpage, April 19, 2018.

---

[26] U.S. Census Bureau, "County Business Patterns: 2016," webpage, April 19, 2018.

Most of the firms that have a large number of employed drivers are not involved in movement of goods for other customers or moving the types of large items demanded in reconstruction projects; they appear to be associated with firms that require handling of their own freight. For example, the largest firms in Puerto Rico by number of truck drivers are

- Vaqueria Tres Monjitas INC: milk products
- Consolidated Waste Services LLC: waste services
- Holsum de Puerto Rico: bread and other food
- PJ Rosaly Enterprises INC: trucking and logistics
- Pan Pepin INC: bread and other food
- Easeway de Puerto Rico CORP: commercial vehicle rental
- ARB INC: waste services.

This list includes all firms with more than 100 employed drivers; a couple of them may be involved in moving large freight items, but the other firms are illustrative examples of the other services that truck drivers may be associated with, other than moving cargo out of the Port of San Juan.

Trucking firms are located mostly in the vicinity of San Juan, and many others are located along the north coast of Puerto Rico (Figure 3.10).

Figure 3.10. Geographic Location of Trucking Firms in Puerto Rico

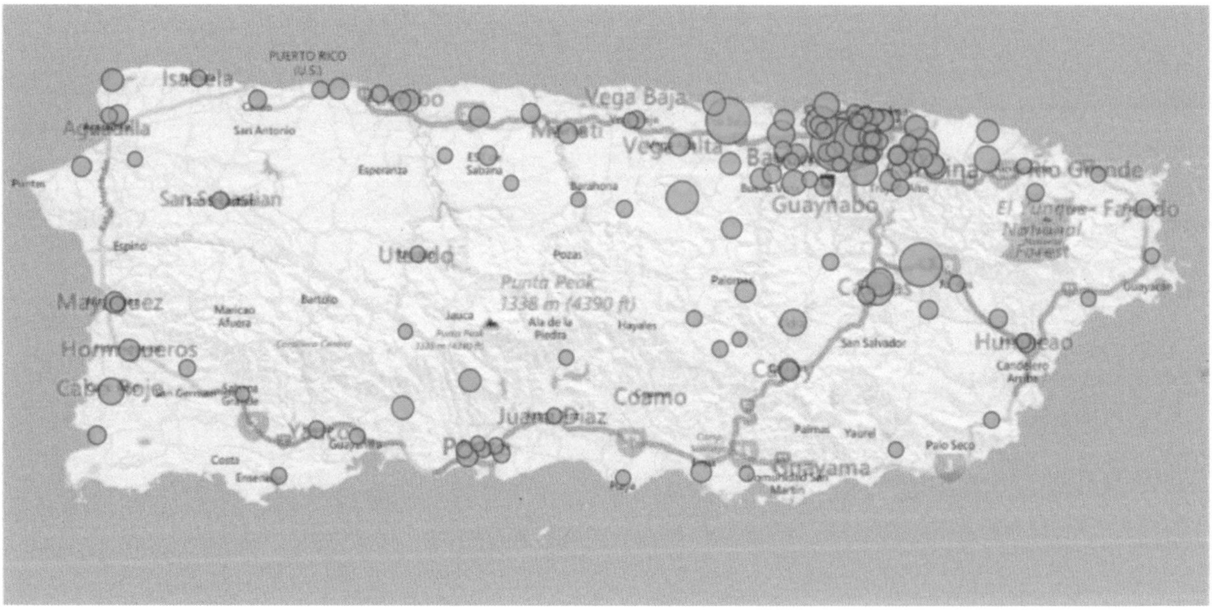

SOURCE: U.S. Census Bureau, April 19, 2018.
NOTE: Size of trucking firms is indicated by the size of the icon; larger circles indicate more employees in the firm.

U.S. Census Federal Motor Carrier Safety Administration 2019

The U.S. Department of Transportation (DOT) reports 6,260 individuals and 6,673 power units (trucks) with DOT trucking licenses in Puerto Rico in 2019.[27]

U.S. Bureau of Labor Statistics 2018

There are 8,130 individuals employed as heavy and tractor-trailer truck drivers in Puerto Rico.[28] Truck drivers in Puerto Rico are the lowest paid truck drivers in the United States. The average hourly wage in Puerto Rico is $9.41. The national average is $21.39, and the lowest tenth percentile nationally is $13.22 hourly.

From these sources and the diverse perspectives of the truck driver occupation on Puerto Rico, it is possible to observe that many of the drivers who will be employed to move cargo from the port to locations in Puerto Rico will work for small businesses, which are largely clustered in the San Juan vicinity. The presence of small trucking businesses, and the lack of large fleet operators, will make it more challenging to coordinate efforts within Puerto Rico. Coordinated recruitment and training support could aid in growing the occupation. Organizing in a collective way could alleviate congestion at the Port of San Juan and across the roadways.

Employment Challenges Facing the U.S. Trucking Industry and Implications for Puerto Rico

As recovery projects in Puerto Rico are funded and executed, incoming cargo shipments are expected to increase substantially. At a $10 billion annual rate of spending on projects similar to the recovery plan COAs, the economy of Puerto Rico is expected to require an additional 2,300 drivers beyond those currently employed (many of whom will be directly employed moving cargo from the ports and around the island). The ability to employ the additional drivers required could be affected by current and projected shortages of drivers in the United States. In 2019 the shortage is expected to exceed 71,000 truck drivers, according to the American Trucking Associations,[29] and that number is expected to increase over the coming years. Relative to the CONUS, Puerto Rico is at a disadvantage because wages for such jobs are 50-percent lower in Puerto Rico than in the United States.

Employers in the CONUS are using several strategies to improve recruitment of new workers that could apply to prospective employers in Puerto Rico. These employers are actively looking

---

[27] U.S. Census Federal Motor Carrier Safety Administration, Safety Measurement System, Motor Carrier Census Information for 2010, undated.

[28] U.S. Department of Labor, Bureau of Labor Statistics, Labor Force Statistics from the Current Population Survey, January 18, 2019.

[29] Bob Costello, *Truck Driver Shortage Analysis 2015*, American Trucking Associations, October 2017.

beyond the "traditional" labor pool of potential workers to recruit women and younger drivers, and they are trying to target receptive demographics, such as veterans.[30]

Women and young people are underrepresented in trucking. Women make up only 6 percent of commercial truckers.[31] The median age of commercial truck drivers is 47, compared with a median age of 42 for all employees.[32] Some employers are specifically targeting these two groups as an untapped labor source.

Several strategies are suggested to increase success in programs for recruiting more women drivers: use ads that appeal to women as well as men, employ women in management roles, consider women when selecting truck specifications, address concerns about security specific to women, and revisit discrimination and harassment policies and training. The Bennett International Group, a woman-owned carrier, has launched such a program, called Bennett Women in the Driver's Seat.[33]

Companies are also targeting young drivers, as they are also underrepresented in the trucking industry. But their inclusion can be challenging. Brenny Transportation has instituted a 17-week training program, including mentoring and feedback sessions, for drivers as young as 18 who possess a commercial learner's permit.[34] Drivers under 21 years of age face challenges driving trucks in the CONUS, as they are able to drive interstate routes only after they turn 21, and insurance companies often have policies that are preferential toward drivers older than 21. The strategy to employ younger drivers could be even more useful in Puerto Rico, since there is no interstate commerce on the island and no current legal barriers to the usefulness of young drivers there.

Employers have also targeted veterans of the armed services. This population is well suited to carriers in several respects. Many were heavy equipment drivers themselves during their enlistment. Also, soldiers leaving the military are often at an ideal age for trucking, since many soldiers come out of a four-year enlistment at 22 years old and have no increased difficulty in getting insured.

Employers are also using additional compensation strategies outside of increasing regular wages, such as increased benefits and signing bonuses. Others are assisting new drivers with deferred payments of the classes required to qualify for operator licenses and insurance coverage, although these classes can be available at community colleges and qualify for financial aid.

There are also efforts at the national level to combat commercial truck driver shortages. Some drivers blame shortages on recent regulations requiring electronic logging devices and

---

[30] Deborah Lockridge, "Expanding the Driver Pool," *Truckinginfo.com*, March 2015.

[31] U.S. Department of Labor, "Occupations by Gender Shares of Employment," 2011.

[32] U.S. Department of Labor, January 18, 2019.

[33] Lockridge, 2015.

[34] Lockridge, 2015.

rules that went into effect in 2013 requiring drivers to drive only for 11 hours within a 14-hour window, after which 10 hours of time off must be taken.[35] Time spent waiting to load and unload cargo that exceeds 3 hours will impinge on the 11-hour window that drivers have available to drive, ultimately reducing their pay.

One of the biggest challenges for recruitment in the industry in the CONUS does not apply in Puerto Rico. In the CONUS, full truckload drivers are often expected to stay on the road for weeks to facilitate fulfillment of long-distance routes. New arrangements are being created in which multiple drivers may cooperate for routes, in order to limit the maximum distance each driver must be from his or her home. However, the limited size of the main island of Puerto Rico limits the length of trucking routes in Puerto Rico, making it unnecessary for drivers there to spend long periods of time away from home. It may be possible to exploit this factor, along with other selling points specific to Puerto Rico, when seeking to recruit new truckers or to hire experienced truckers from the CONUS.

Conclusions

Economic analyses indicate that with a baseline estimate of $10 billion in annual recovery spending, 2,300 additional truckers will be needed—5,800 if recovery funds are spent at a rate of $25 billion per year. (Not all of these truckers will be employed moving cargo from the seaborne supply chain into Puerto Rico, but a sizable portion will.) The principal constraints in the roadways will be traffic congestion in San Juan and its vicinity, and possibly last mile transportation to interior areas of the island. The findings from the capacity models indicate that except during peak hours, the highways of Puerto Rico that are outside San Juan have enough capacity to absorb additional demand caused by recovery efforts without significant delays; off-peak, highways outside San Juan can handle 1,000–2,000 additional trucks per hour before very high risk of congestion. Highways in San Juan are likely to be congested even in off-peak hours, but these will likely experience delays on the order of hours, as they have the capacity to accommodate an increase of 100–400 trucks per hour. Moreover, at current loadings and inventory ratings, most bridges along the highway network should be able to sustain additional traffic, although some will require maintenance soon.

An analysis of sectors across the Puerto Rico economy reveals that enhancing the labor supply will be crucial to supporting recovery efforts.[36] The main requirement for the seaborne supply chain at the outset of the recovery will be the availability of truckers, and this should be addressed specifically. It may take some time for the labor market to adjust and attract truck

---

[35] Steve Banker, "The Truck Driver Shortage Can Be Solved by Paying Drivers for All the Work They Do," *Forbes.com*, April 30, 2018.

[36] RAND Corporation, Spring 2019.

drivers, as there is a current shortage of truck drivers in the United States.[37] Possible policy options include working with U.S. interagency partners such as the Department of Labor, and workforce training, development, and retention programs designed to increase employment of key occupations in Puerto Rico. To support the logistics capacity of Puerto Rico as materials are imported for recovery projects, the availability of trucks and truck drivers is fundamental.

Once trucking is available, the main transportation challenges will be conditions in San Juan, last mile transportation, and dynamism in highway conditions such as maintenance and weather. San Juan, where the first miles of transportation will be incurred, exhibits high-volume conditions throughout the day. This will cause travel delays and inconvenience, but only in terms of hours. Last mile transportation to rural areas in mountainous regions will require additional preplanning, such as use of lighter trucks or additional handling and transferring of freight. Finally, road conditions are always changing, and weather, construction, and maintenance may temporarily alter capacities.

The analysis of potential travel conditions on the road network suggests that coordinating projects will be beneficial. Smoothing material demands for truckers and managing pickups and drop-offs around peak times on roads would improve material throughput and cost.

---

[37] Thomas Black, "With Truckers in Control, Money Talks and Toilets Sparkle," *Bloomberg*, May 11, 2018.

4. Conclusions and Recommendations

Conclusions

The Puerto Rico Recovery Plan seeks over $130 billion, to be spent over 11 years. One of the focuses of the plan is on physical construction projects. During execution of those projects, there will be a sizable increase in the amount of large, heavy materials that are imported to Puerto Rico by the seaborne supply chain.

Our research has examined the ability of Puerto Rico's seaborne supply chain, including its ports and road network, to process the increased seaborne cargo shipments required to support the recovery effort projects. Those analyses used a modeling approach to project the additional transportation burden of the increase in cargo from the seaport to the road network of the island. We also collected and synthesized lessons learned from experiences during the aftermath of Hurricane Maria, in which there was both an increase in the amount of incoming seaborne containerized cargo (in the form of relief shipments) and a shortfall in the amount of trucking available, conditions that may occur as a result of increases to incoming seaborne cargo shipments to support recovery efforts.

Our analyses have led to the following insights.

Findings

1. Terminal operators of the Port of San Juan have optimized their operations to deal with steady-state levels of demand, which are very consistent. Profit motives limit the operators' incentive to prepare for demand surge conditions (and as they are private-sector firms, government agencies have limited ability and scope of mission to influence their management). However, as there are multiple terminal operators, and they are profit-seeking firms, it can be expected that they will grow their operations to achieve higher capacity if demand is consistently increased and they have sufficient time to react. The degree to which cargo is slowed as it moves through the ports depends on the size and rate of the increase in demand, the lead-time notice given to terminal operators, and the availability of trucking. If truck shipments cannot keep up with incoming containers, operators will be forced to store containers at terminal yards. As storage yards become more congested, outgoing truck shipments from the terminals will suffer worse delays. These delays may, in turn, worsen the problem, which stems from fewer outgoing container shipments than incoming arrivals.

   Since there is no way to avoid using the San Juan port, as no other port is equipped to deal with large-scale container volume, the only option to mitigate the bottleneck is to increase the port's capacity. The key capacity constraint in the case of the Port of San Juan is not in pier berths and quay cranes but in material handling equipment and yard space to store containers. The terminal operators may be able to arrange for access to more equipment if needed. For best results, if increases in demand are managed to be smooth and communicated with sufficient lead time to terminal operators, the operators can ensure that equipment will be in place when it is needed. However, it is up to the PRPA to make land or space available for lease.

2. It can take a month or more for port operators (or many types of firms) to change business and operating policies to adapt to surges in demand and integrate additional capacity in a useful and effective way. In addition to procuring reach-tuggers and other equipment, it may be difficult to scale labor to meet a surge, bringing a few selected staff from other locations operated by the same companies, and turning to the general labor economy of Puerto Rico.
3. Separate economic analyses indicate that with $10 billion in annual recovery spending, 2,300 additional truckers will be needed. It is unclear at what pace the demand for trucking services will proceed at the beginning of the implementation plan, as this will first require submission and approval of construction projects and procurement of the necessary contractors, which could take several months or more. This will require the labor market to adjust and requires procuring vehicles, training and licensing new drivers, attracting truck drivers at a given wage (as wages in Puerto Rico for this work are about half of what they would be in the CONUS),[1] or hiring ones from the CONUS. It takes approximately seven to nine weeks to earn a commercial driver's license by attending a commercial trucking school full time.[2] In addition to recruitment and transporting drivers and trucks to the island, the full process can take several months. Recruitment efforts could be complicated by the continued shortage of trucking labor in the CONUS. In 2019, driver shortages are expected to exceed 71,000 workers,[3] in spite of steadily increasing average salaries. Since procurement of trucking services is a prerequisite to utilizing the road network, potential lags may occur here before the actual infrastructure is used.
4. If trucking is available, the main transportation challenges will be conditions in San Juan, last mile transportation, and dynamism in highway conditions such as maintenance and weather. San Juan—where the first miles of transportation will be incurred—exhibits high-volume conditions throughout the day. This will cause travel delays and inconvenience, but only in terms of hours. Last mile transportation to rural areas in mountainous regions will require additional preplanning, such as use of lighter trucks or additional handling and transferring of freight.
5. If each additional trucker employed increases the number of trucks on the road by one, the Puerto Rico road network outside San Juan can accommodate this additional demand. Off-peak, the highways outside San Juan can handle 1,000–2,000 additional trucks per hour before there is a very high risk of congestion. This capacity is expected to be sufficient for the amount of recovery activity associated with $10 billion in annual recovery spending. Highways in San Juan are more limited. Highways in San Juan are more likely to be congested even in off-peak hours, but these will likely experience only minor delays and inconvenience, and they can accommodate up to a sizable 100–400 trucks per hour. Provided that additional material is released over several hours at off-peak times, highways near San Juan,

[1] RAND Corporation, Spring 2019.

[2] J. F. Morgan et al., 2011.

[3] Costello, 2017.

including PR-18, PR-22, PR-52, PR-26, and PR-30, will also have sufficient capacity. Moreover, bridges along the highway network should be able to sustain the additional traffic, although some will require maintenance soon. These findings assume that population levels do not significantly increase and that traffic patterns do not change greatly.

6. While the island's road network can accommodate the expected increase in trucking associated with the recovery plan, the burden of a 29-percent increase in trucking could introduce significant delays or exacerbate existing delays if introduced into the road network outside San Juan during peak hours.

Recommendations

There are several actions that FEMA could take directly or facilitate to mitigate the potential problems identified above. HSOAC offers the following recommendations:

- Coordination between FEMA and the port terminal operators may enable the terminal operators to prepare effectively for managing increased container shipments by arranging for access to more material handling equipment (especially reach-tuggers) as soon as it is needed.
- The PRPA should make more space available for use as container yard adjacent to or near the Crowley Maritime terminal. Warehouse 21, which is damaged beyond repair, could be taken down and used as yard space. Warehouse 22 could also be taken down and used for container storage during a surge.
- The PRPA should also avoid using potential cargo yard space that is near a cargo terminal for debris storage after a natural disaster. Instead, the PRPA should find locations away from the port terminals to store garbage and debris, to preserve alternative future options for use of the space by cargo terminals.
- The analysis of potential travel conditions on the road network suggests that coordinating projects will be beneficial. The government of Puerto Rico could direct an office to gather information about recovery projects and make the information accessible. By that means, municipalities and government agencies that contract for work to be performed can time projects to be complementary. For instance, recovery projects in a geographic area that inhibit services to residents (such as requiring streets to be closed or water or power to be turned off) can be performed simultaneously, to minimize the time that residents are inconvenienced. Or, recovery projects that are in a geographic area and require large amounts of materials to be moved (such as large-scale construction projects) can be performed in sequence to minimize the amount of heavy trucks added to traffic flow at the same time. This measure would smooth demands for truckers to move material. Similarly, managing pickups and drop-offs to avoid peak times on roads would improve material throughput and cost of transportation.
- FEMA and U.S. government agencies should focus on workforce capacity building in Puerto Rico, including truck drivers, to address logistics challenges ahead of execution of recovery plan projects.

References

Banker, Steve, "The Truck Driver Shortage Can Be Solved by Paying Drivers for All the Work They Do," *Forbes.com*, April 30, 2018. As of April 18, 2019:
https://www.forbes.com/sites/stevebanker/2018/04/30/addressing-the-driver-shortage-by-paying-drivers-for-all-the-work-they-do/#134778d01f07

Black, Thomas, "With Truckers in Control, Money Talks and Toilets Sparkle," *Bloomberg*, May 11, 2018. As of April 10, 2019:
https://www.bloomberg.com/news/articles/2018-05-11/truck-shortage-has-shippers-luring-u-s-drivers-with-coffee-tv

Brinkman, B., "Operations Systems of Container Terminals: A Compendious Overview," in J. Böse, ed., *Handbook of Terminal Planning*, New York: Springer, 2011, pp. 25–39.

Bureau of Economic Analysis, *RIMS II: An Essential Tool for Regional Developers and Planners*, December 2013. As of April 18, 2019:
https://www.bea.gov/sites/default/files/methodologies/RIMSII_User_Guide.pdf

Central Office for Recovery, Reconstruction and Resiliency, *Transformation and Innovation in the Wake of Devastation: An Economic and Disaster Recovery Plan for Puerto Rico*, August 8, 2018. As of April 8, 2019:
http://www.p3.pr.gov/assets/pr-transformation-innovation-plan-congressional-submission-080818.pdf

Costello, Bob, *Truck Driver Shortage Analysis 2015*, American Trucking Associations, 2017.

"Crowley Establishes Flow of Relief Cargo into Puerto Rico Following Hurricane Maria," *Crowley Maritime*, September 22, 2017. As of February 8, 2019:
http://www.crowley.com/news-and-media/press-releases/crowley-establishes-flow-of-relief-cargo-into-puerto-rico-following-hurricane-maria/

Domonoske, Camila, "In Puerto Rico, Containers Full of Goods Sit Undistributed at Ports," *National Public Radio*, September 28, 2017. As of February 7, 2019:
https://www.npr.org/sections/thetwo-way/2017/09/28/554297787/puerto-rico-relief-goods-sit-undistributed-at-ports

Departamento de Transportación de Obras Públicas, "General Design Criteria," chapter 1 in *Design Manual*, Puerto Rico Highway and Transportation Authority, 1979. As of April 18, 2019:
http://www.dtop.gov.pr/pdf/129-Chapter_01.pdf

DTOP—*See* Departamento de Transportación de Obras Públicas.

Erickson, Bo, "After Hurricane Maria, Fuel Requests by Walmart Stores in Puerto Rico Went Unanswered," *CBS News*, 2017. As of February 7, 2019:

https://www.cbsnews.com/news/after-hurricane-maria-fuel-requests-by-walmart-stores-in-puerto-rico-went-unanswered/

Federal Highway Administration, "Tables of Frequently Requested NBI Information," undated. As of April 19, 2019: https://www.fhwa.dot.gov/bridge/britab.cfm

———, *Recording and Coding Guide for the Structure Inventory and Appraisal of the Nation's Bridges*, Washington, D.C., Report FHWA-PD-96-001, 1995. As of April 19, 2019: https://www.fhwa.dot.gov/bridge/mtguide.pdf

———, "National Bridge Inventory," 2017. As of February 7, 2019: https://www.fhwa.dot.gov/bridge/nbi/ascii2017.cfm

FHWA—*See* Federal Highway Administration.

Galarza, Javier Rodriguez, "Population Density of Puerto Rico," Wikipedia.org. As of May 7, 2019: https://en.wikipedia.org/wiki/File:Population_Density,_PR,_2000_(sample).jpg

Giel, Dawn, Contessa Brewer, and Lori Ann LaRocco, "Puerto Rico, Short on Fuel, Cannot Deliver Food and Medicine to the Victims of Hurricane Maria," *CNBC*, September 28, 2017. As of February 7, 2019: https://www.cnbc.com/2017/09/28/puerto-ricos-fuel-supply-breaks-down-in-the-wake-of-marias-devastation.html

Google, "Distance Maps API," undated. As of February 5, 2019: https://developers.google.com/maps/documentation/distance-matrix/intro

Hartmann, S., J. Pohlmann, and A. Schönknecht, "Simulation of Container Ship Arrivals and Quay Occupation," in J. Böse, ed., *Handbook of Terminal Planning*, New York: Springer, 2011, pp. 135–154.

Lagoudis, I. N., and J. Rice, Jr., "Revisiting Port Capacity: A Practical Method for Investment and Policy Decisions," Proceedings, ECONSHIP, Chios, Greece, 2011.

Lockridge, Deborah, "Expanding the Driver Pool," *Truckinginfo.com*, March 1, 2015. As of April 18, 2019: https://www.truckinginfo.com/155992/expanding-the-driver-pool

Margiotta, R., and S. Washburn, *Simplified Highway Capacity Calculation Method for the Highway Performance Monitoring System*, Report for Federal Highway Administration, PL-18-003, Washington, D.C.: Federal Highway Administration, October 2017. As of April 18, 2019: https://www.fhwa.dot.gov/policyinformation/pubs/pl18003/hpms_cap.pdf

Morgan, J. F., Scott Tidwell, Alejandra Medina, and Myra Blanco, "On the Training and Testing of Entry-Level Commercial Motor Vehicle Drivers," *Accident Analysis and Prevention*, Vol. 43, No. 4, 2011, pp. 1400–1407.

Pipoli, R., "Puerto Rico's Ponce Port Completes $250 Million Upgrade, Eyes Caribbean Market," *Latin Business Daily*, September 7, 2015. As of May 11, 2018: https://latinbusinessdaily.com/stories/510636837-puerto-rico-s-ponce-port-completes-250-million-upgrade-eyes-caribbean-market

Port of the Americas, "About the Project," webpage, December 7, 2011.

RAND Corporation, "Supporting Puerto Rico's Disaster Recovery Planning," webpage, undated. As of Spring 2019: https://www.rand.org/hsoac/puerto-rico-recovery.html

Transportation Research Board, *Highway Capacity Manual: HCM 2010*, Washington, D.C., 2010.

U.S. Census Bureau, "County Business Patterns: 2016," webpage, April 19, 2018. As of May 6, 2019: https://www.census.gov/data/datasets/2016/econ/cbp/2016-cbp.html

U.S. Census Federal Motor Carrier Safety Administration, Safety Measurement System, Motor Carrier Census Information for 2010, undated. As of February 22, 2019: https://ai.fmcsa.dot.gov/SMS/Tools/Downloads.aspx

U.S. Code, Title 42, Section 5121, Chapter 68, Disaster Relief, November 23, 1988. As of July 12, 2019: https://www.fema.gov/media-library-data/1519395888776-af5f95a1a9237302af7e3fd5b0d07d71/StaffordAct.pdf

U.S. Department of Labor, "Occupations by Gender Shares of Employment," 2011.

U.S. Department of Labor, Bureau of Labor Statistics, Labor Force Statistics from the Current Population Survey, January 18, 2019. As of May 6, 2019: https://www.bls.gov/cps/

U.S. Department of Transportation Maritime Administration, "U.S. Waterborne Foreign Container Trade by U.S. Customs Ports 2000–2017," 2017. As of April 18, 2019: https://www.maritime.dot.gov/data-reports/data-statistics/us-waterborne-foreign-container-trade-us-customs-ports-2000-%E2%80%93-2017

U.S. Government Accountability Office, *Puerto Rico, Characteristics of the Island's Maritime Trade and Potential Effects of Modifying the Jones Act*, GAO-13-260, Washington, D.C., March 2013.